Reading Literature:

Fiction, Poetry, and Exercises
Based on the Common Core
State Standards

Level
10

Prestwick House

Senior Editor:
Paul Moliken

Writer:
Jack Turner, Ph.D.

Cover and Text Design:
Jen Mendoza

Layout and Production:
Jeremy Clark

Prestwick House

© 2014 by Prestwick House, Inc.

Printed in the United States of America.

ISBN: 978-1-62019-157-6

Item No. 309477

TABLE OF CONTENTS

READING
SELECTIONS

Bjørnstjerne Bjørnson

The Father

INTRODUCTION

The Father

This story, first published in 1860, is classified as a "peasant tale," a type of folktale. The main character, while a peasant in terms of social class, is also a successful farmer. Though the setting is rural Norway in the mid-nineteenth century, "The Father" is universal in its appeal and popularity, partly because it is short, easy to understand, and centered on basic human concerns, but mostly due to its moral and philosophical depth. It closely resembles a biblical parable and has a similar, long-lasting impact.

Bjørnstjerne Bjørnson

The winner of the 1903 Nobel Prize for Literature, Bjørnstjerne Bjørnson was born on December 8, 1832 in Kvikne, a village about 230 miles north of Oslo, Norway. Known by English readers primarily for his stories about rural life, he was also a prominent playwright and poet who was, at one time, as famous as his countryman, friend, and fellow playwright Henrik Ibsen (1828-1906). Both are included in the so-called "Big Four" Norwegian writers of the nineteenth century, along with Alexander Kielland and Jonas Lie.

In 1849, Bjørnson left for Christiania (now Oslo) to study at a college preparatory school, where he became friends with Ibsen, who was also attending the school. Drawn to the world of the theater, he soon drifted away from his formal education and became a critic of drama and literature for the local newspaper. Becoming active and successful in theater circles, in 1859, Bjørnson joined Ibsen in founding the Norwegian Society for Theater, Music, and Language. Meanwhile, Bjørnson had also become a popular writer of stories, many of them set in the scenic lands of his boyhood, as are his first two novels, *Synnøve Solbakken* (1857; translated as *Trust and Trial*) and *Arne* (1859). An 1859 poem by Bjørnson, "Ja, vi elsker dette landet" ("Yes, We Love This Land"), was set to music and became the Norwegian national anthem.

Bjørnson's later years were filled with the writing of many plays and a vigorous involvement with politics, as he strongly championed the independence, cultural legacy, and unique identity of Norway, the rights of peasants and common workers, and equality for women. He had become used to spending winters in Paris, one of his favorite cities, and he had also gone there to receive treatment for a heart condition. It was ultimately unsuccessful, however, and he died on April 26, 1910.

The Father
Bjørnstjerne Bjørnson (1860)

I

THE MAN WHOSE story is here to be told was the wealthiest and most influential person in his parish; his name was Thord Överaas. He appeared in the priest's study one day, tall and earnest.

"I have gotten a son," said he, "and I wish to present him for baptism."

"What shall his name be?"

"Finn,—after my father."

5 "And the sponsors?"

They were mentioned, and proved to be the best men and women of Thord's relations in the parish.

"Is there anything else?" inquired the priest, and looked up. The peasant hesitated a little.

"I should like very much to have him baptized by himself," said he, finally.

"That is to say on a week-day?"

10 "Next Saturday, at twelve o'clock noon."

"Is there anything else?" inquired the priest,

"There is nothing else;" and the peasant twirled his cap, as though he were about to go.

Then the priest rose. "There is yet this, however," said he, and walking toward Thord, he took him by the hand and looked gravely into his eyes: "God grant that the child may become a blessing to you!"

II

ONE DAY SIXTEEN years later, Thord stood once more in the priest's study.

"Really, you carry your age astonishingly well, Thord," said the priest; for he saw no change whatever in the man.

"That is because I have no troubles," replied Thord. To this the priest said nothing, but after a while he asked: "What is your pleasure this evening?"

"I have come this evening about that son of mine who is to be confirmed to-morrow."

5   "He is a bright boy."

"I did not wish to pay the priest until I heard what number the boy would have when he takes his place in the church to-morrow."

"He will stand number one."

"So I have heard; and here are ten dollars for the priest."

"Is there anything else I can do for you?" inquired the priest, fixing his eyes on Thord.

10   "There is nothing else."

Thord went out.

III

EIGHT YEARS MORE rolled by, and then one day a noise was heard outside of the priest's study, for many men were approaching, and at their head was Thord, who entered first.

The priest looked up and recognized him.

"You come well attended this evening, Thord," said he.

Banns: the official announcement of a marriage

"I am here to request that the **banns** may be published for my son: he is about to marry Karen Storliden, daughter of Gudmund, who stands here beside me."

5   "Why, that is the richest girl in the parish."

"So they say," replied the peasant, stroking back his hair with one hand.

The priest sat a while as if in deep thought, then entered the names in his book, without making any comments, and the men wrote their signatures underneath. Thord laid three dollars on the table.

"One is all I am to have," said the priest.

"I know that very well; but he is my only child; I want to do it handsomely."

10   The priest took the money.

"This is now the third time, Thord, that you have come here on your son's account."

"But now I am through with him," said Thord, and folding up his pocket-book he said farewell and walked away.

The men slowly followed him.

A **fortnight** later, the father and son were rowing across the lake, one calm, still day, to Storliden to make arrangements for the wedding.

15   "This **thwart** is not secure," said the son, and stood up to straighten the seat on which he was sitting.

At the same moment the board he was standing on slipped from under him; he threw out his arms, uttered a shriek, and fell overboard.

"Take hold of the oar!" shouted the father, springing to his feet, and holding out the oar.

But when the son had made a couple of efforts he grew stiff.

"Wait a moment!" cried the father, and began to row toward his son.

20   Then the son rolled over on his back, gave his father one long look, and sank.

Thord could scarcely believe it; he held the boat still, and stared at the spot where his son had gone down, as though he must surely come to the surface again. There rose some bubbles, then some more, and finally one large one that burst; and the lake lay there as smooth and bright as a mirror again.

For three days and three nights people saw the father rowing round and round the spot, without taking either food or sleep; he was dragging the lake for the body of his son. And toward morning of the third day he found it, and carried it in his arms up over the hills to his gard.

IV

IT MIGHT HAVE been about a year from that day, when the priest, late one autumn evening, heard some one in the passage outside of the door, carefully trying to find the latch. The priest opened the door, and in walked a tall, thin man, with bowed form and white hair. The priest looked long at him before he recognized him. It was Thord.

"Are you out walking so late?" said the priest, and stood still in front of him.

"Ah, yes! it is late," said Thord, and took a seat.

Fortnight: a period of 14 days

Thwart: a crosspiece in a boat that can be used as a seat by a rower

The number three is important in Christian symbolism because of the Trinity (God, Jesus Christ, and the Holy Spirit); Christ performed three functions while on Earth, namely prophet, priest, and king. He rose from his grave on the third day. In addition, the disciple Peter, fearing for his life, denied three times that he knew Christ. There are many other instances in which three is a number with special significance.

The priest sat down also, as though waiting. A long, long silence followed. At last Thord said,—

5   "I have something with me that I should like to give to the poor; I want it to be invested as a legacy in my son's name."

He rose, laid some money on the table, and sat down again. The priest counted it.

"It is a great deal of money," said he.

"It is half the price of my gard. I sold it to-day."

The priest sat long in silence. At last he asked, but gently,—

10   "What do you propose to do now, Thord?"

"Something better."

They sat there for a while, Thord with downcast eyes, the priest with his eyes fixed on Thord. Presently the priest said, slowly and softly,—

"I think your son has at last brought you a true blessing."

QUESTIONS

1. What can you logically infer about the protagonist, Thord Överaas, based on the text of part I?

2. In part II, when Thord explains his youthful appearance by saying, "That is because I have no troubles," the priest remains silent for a while. How do you think the author intended this silence to be interpreted?

3. Soon afterward, Thord says, "I did not wish to pay the priest until I heard what number the boy would have when he takes his place in the church to-morrow" (for his Christian confirmation). After the priest says that Finn will be the first in line, Thord pays him ten dollars. What are the connotations of this exchange?

4. Part III shows the main character asking for a third favor from the priest. This time, Thord wants the church to publish the "banns" (the announcement of a marriage) for his son and "the richest girl in the parish," as the priest refers to her. Thord agrees that she is and arrogantly smooths his hair back with his hand. Then the priest is silent again, this time "as if in deep thought." What can you infer from what the priest does not say?

5. Although the customary price of the priest's publishing of the banns is only a dollar, Thord gives him three, saying that Finn "is my only child, and I want to do it handsomely." The priest then notes that Thord has come to see him three times on his son's behalf. This visit also occurs in part III, which ends with Thord searching "three days and three nights" for his son's body. On "the third day he found it." What effect does this heavily symbolic structure have on the story?

6. Near the end, after the priest finally recognizes the "tall, thin man, with bowed form and white hair" as Thord, the priest asks if he is "working so late." Thord replies, "Ah, yes! It is late." In this situation, what are the connotations of Thord's words, and how do they impact the meaning and tone?

7. When Thord sits down, the priest is completely quiet, and his silence lasts a long time. What can be logically inferred from his silence this time?

8. Based on the priest's final words to Thord and the man's agreement with them, determine the main theme of the short story. Then decide on a subtheme and show how the two interact and build on one another to add complexity to what is, on the surface, a very simple folktale.

9. What significance, multiple meanings, and connotations can you derive from the title of the story?

Maria Edgeworth

The Purple Jar

INTRODUCTION

The Purple Jar

Edgeworth's most famous short story, this instructive, symbolic tale about the results of a little girl's purchasing decision, was originally published in a collection called *The Parent's Assistant* in 1796. Edgeworth later included it in *Early Lessons* (1801). Her father, Richard Lovell Edgeworth, was a well-known author, inventor, and politician, and he insisted on reading and approving all her stories before she could publish them or read them to any of her many siblings. When she became a novelist, she still valued her father's opinion and even credited him as the inspiration behind her entire literary career. In 1900, a painting called "Rosamund and the Purple Jar" was exhibited by Henry Tonks, a well-respected English artist and teacher. It is now owned by the Tate Gallery in London.

Maria Edgeworth

Maria Edgeworth was born on January 1, 1768, in a village in Oxfordshire, England. She is known for her social realism, which was ahead of its time, and her strict educational philosophy that vigorously encouraged the development of a child's inner strength and independence. As one of the first realistic writers, she was a considerable force in the development of the novel. Maintaining her own independence throughout her life, she influenced such leading writers as William Makepeace Thackeray, Sir Walter Scott, and Jane Austen. Scott became a close friend, and Austen sent Edgeworth an advance copy of the novel *Emma* (1815). Even the Russian novelist Ivan Turgenev was a strong admirer and reportedly said that if he had not read her writing, he may not have become a writer himself.

Edgeworth's first novel, *Castle Rackrent* (1800), which she secretly and anonymously published without her father's editing, is a landmark in British fiction. It is the first historical novel, for example, as well as the first saga novel, and it is also the first to feature an unreliable narrator who is also a character. *Castle Rackrent* shows the excesses of the Irish ruling class with no embellishments or saving graces. As in her other Irish novels, it also depicts the plight of the Irish peasants, whom she championed and assisted throughout her life, especially during the disastrous Potato Famine that began in 1845.

From her first publication, *Letters for Literary Ladies* (1795), through her children's stories and all of her novels, Edgeworth attempted to further the education of women and teach children practical lessons. Her published stories and novels did not veer away from reality and made her an uncompromising, effective, and compassionate leader in both these areas. After working for years to ease the stress and hunger of less-fortunate people during the famine, Edgeworth died of a heart attack on May 22, 1849.

The Purple Jar
Maria Edgeworth (1796)

ROSAMOND, A LITTLE GIRL of about seven years old, was walking with her mother in the streets of London. As she passed along, she looked in at the windows of several shops, and she saw a great variety of different sorts of things, of which she did not know the use, or even the names. She wished to stop to look at them; but there was a great number of people in the streets, and a great many carts and carriages and wheelbarrows, and she was afraid to let go her mother's hand.

"Oh! mother, how happy I should be," said she, as she passed a toy-shop, "if I had all these pretty things!"

"What, all! Do you wish for them all, Rosamond?"

"Yes, mamma, all."

5 As she spoke, they came to a **milliner**'s shop; the windows were hung with ribbons, and lace, and **festoons** of artificial flowers.

Milliner: a maker or seller of hats

Festoons: ribbons

"Oh! mamma, what beautiful roses! Won't you buy some of them?"

"No, my dear."

"Why?"

"Because I don't want them, my dear."

10 They went a little farther, and they came to another shop, which caught Rosamond's eye. It was a jeweler's shop; and there were a great many pretty baubles, ranged in drawers behind glass.

"Mamma, you'll buy some of these?"

"Which of them, Rosamond?"

"Which? I don't know which; but any of them, for they are all pretty."

"Yes, they are all pretty; but of what use would they be to me?"

15 "Use! Oh, I'm sure you could find some use or other, if you would only buy them first."

"But I would rather find out the use first."

Rosamond was very sorry that her mother

Chemist: a pharmacist

wanted nothing. Presently, however, they came to a shop, which appeared to her far more beautiful than the rest. It was a **chemist**'s shop; but she did not know that.

"Oh, mother! oh!" cried she, pulling her mother's hand. "Look! Look! Blue, green, red, yellow, and purple! Oh, mamma, what beautiful things! Won't you buy some of these?"

Still her mother answered as before, "What use would they be to me, Rosamond?"

20   "You might put flowers in them, mamma, and they would look so pretty on the chimney-piece. I wish I had one of them."

"You have a flower-vase," said her mother; "and that is not for flowers."

"But I could use it for a flower-vase, mamma, you know."

"Perhaps if you were to see it nearer, if you were to examine it, you might be disappointed."

"No, indeed; I'm sure I should not. I should like it exceedingly."

25   Rosamond kept her head turned to look at the purple vase till she could see it no longer.

"Then, mother," said she, after a pause, "perhaps you have no money."

"Yes, I have."

"Dear me! if I had money, I would buy roses, and boxes, and purple flower-pots, and everything." Rosamond was obliged to pause in the midst of her speech.

"Oh, mamma, would you stop a minute for me? I have got a stone in my shoe; it hurts me very much."

30   "How comes there to be a stone in your shoe?"

"Because of this great hole, mamma—it comes in there: my shoes are quite worn out; I wish you'd be so very good as to give me another pair."

"Nay, Rosamond, but I have not money enough to buy shoes, and flower-pots, and boxes, and everything."

Rosamond thought that was a great pity. But now her foot, which had been hurt by the stone, began to give her so much pain that she was obliged to hop every other step, and she could think of nothing else. They came to a shoemaker's shop soon afterwards.

"There! there! mamma, there are shoes—there are little shoes that would just fit me; and you know shoes would be really of use to me."

35   "Yes, so they would, Rosamond. Come in."

She followed her mother into the shop.

Mr. Sole, the shoemaker, had a great many customers, and his shop was full, so they were obliged to wait.

"Well, Rosamond," said her mother, "you don't think this shop so pretty as the rest?"

"No, not nearly; it's black and dark, and there are nothing but shoes all round; and besides, there's a very disagreeable smell."

40   "That smell is the smell of new leather."

"Is it? Oh!" said Rosamond, looking round, "there is a pair of little shoes; they'll just fit me, I'm sure."

"Perhaps they might, but you cannot be sure till you have tried them on, any more than you can be quite sure that you should like the purple vase exceedingly, till you have examined it more attentively."

"Why, I don't know about the shoes, certainly, till I've tried; but, mamma, I'm quite sure I should like the flower-pot."

"Well, which would you rather have, that jar, or a pair of shoes? I will buy either for you."

45   "Dear mamma, thank you—but if you could buy both?"

"No, not both."

"Then the jar, if you please."

"But I should tell you that I shall not give you another pair of shoes this month."

"This month! That's a very long time indeed. You can't think how these hurt me. I believe I'd better have the new shoes—but yet, that purple flower-pot—Oh, indeed, mamma, these shoes are not so very, very bad; I think I might wear them a little longer; and the month will soon be over: I can make them last to the end of the month, can't I? Don't you think so, mamma?"

50   "Nay, my dear, I want you to think for yourself: you will have time enough to consider about it whilst I speak to Mr. Sole about my boots."

Mr. Sole was by this time at leisure; and whilst her mother was speaking to him, Rosamond stood in **profound** meditation, with one shoe on, and the other in her hand.

"Well, my dear, have you decided?"

"Mamma!—Yes—I believe. If you please—I should like the flower-pot; that is, if you won't think me very silly, mamma."

"Why, as to that, I can't promise you, Rosamond; but when you are to judge for yourself, you should choose what will make you the happiest; and then it would not signify who thought you silly."

55   "Then, mamma, if that's all, I'm sure the flower-pot would make me the happiest," said she, putting on her old shoe again; "so I choose the flower-pot."

"Very well, you shall have it: clasp your shoe and come home."

Rosamond clasped her shoe, and ran after her mother: it was not long before the shoe came down at the heel, and many times was she obliged to stop, to take the stones out of her shoe, and often was she obliged to hop with pain; but still the thoughts of the purple flower-pot prevailed, and she persisted in her choice.

When they came to the shop with the large window, Rosamond felt her joy redouble, upon hearing her mother desire the servant, who was with them, to buy the purple jar, and bring it home. He had other commissions, so he did not return with them. Rosamond, as soon as she got in, ran to gather all her own flowers, which she had in a corner of her mother's garden.

"I'm afraid they'll be dead before the flower-pot comes, Rosamond," said her mother to her, when she was coming in with the flowers in her lap.

Profound: intense

Even though Rosamond's family has a servant who is helping them shop, that does not mean that they are in the upper class or have plenty of money. In eighteenth-century London, most middle-class families had at least one servant, and many had more.

60   "No, indeed, mamma, it will come home very soon, I dare say; and shan't I be very happy putting them into the purple flower-pot?"

"I hope so, my dear."

The servant was much longer returning home than Rosamond had expected; but at length he came, and brought with him the long-wished-for jar. The moment it was set down upon the table, Rosamond ran up with an exclamation of joy.

"I may have it now, mamma?"

"Yes, my dear, it is yours."

65   Rosamond poured the flowers from her lap upon the carpet, and seized the purple flower-pot. "Oh, dear mother!" cried she, as soon as she had taken off the top, "but there's something dark in it —it smells very disagreeable: what is in it? I didn't want this black stuff."

"Nor I neither, my dear."

"But what shall I do with it, mamma?"

"That I cannot tell."

"But it will be of no use to me, mamma."

70   "That I can't help."

"But I must pour it out, and fill the flower-pot with water."

"That's as you please, my dear."

"Will you lend me a bowl to pour it into, mamma?"

"That was more than I promised you, my dear; but I will lend you a bowl."

75   The bowl was produced, and Rosamond proceeded to empty the purple vase. But what was her surprise and disappointment, when it was entirely empty, to find that it was no longer a purple vase! It was a plain white glass jar, which had appeared to have that beautiful color merely from the **liquor** with which it had been filled.

Liquor: In this context, the word simply means "liquid."

Little Rosamond burst into tears.

"Why should you cry, my dear?" said her mother; "it will be of as much use to you now as ever for a flower-vase."

"But it won't look so pretty on the chimney-piece. I am sure, if I had known that it was not really purple, I should not have wished to have it so much."

"But didn't I tell you that you had not examined it, and that perhaps you would be disappointed?"

80 "And so I am disappointed indeed. I wish I had believed you beforehand. Now I had much rather have the shoes, for I shall not be able to walk all this month: even walking home that little way hurt me exceedingly. Mamma, I'll give you the flower-pot back again, and that purple stuff and all, if you'll only give me the shoes."

"No, Rosamond, you must abide by your own choice; and now the best thing you can possibly do is to bear your disappointment with good-humor."

"I will bear it as well as I can," said Rosamond, wiping her eyes, and she began slowly and sorrowfully to fill the vase with flowers.

But Rosamond's disappointment did not end here: many were the difficulties and distresses into which her **imprudent** choice brought her before the end of the month. Every day her shoes grew worse and worse, till at last she could neither run, dance, jump, nor walk in them. Whenever Rosamond was called to see anything, she was pulling up her shoes at the heels, and was sure to be too late. Whenever her mother was going out to walk, she could not take Rosamond with her, for Rosamond had no soles to her shoes; and at length, on the very last day of the month, it happened that her father proposed to take her and her brother to a glass-house which she had long wished to see. She was very happy; but, when she was quite ready, had her hat and gloves on, and was making haste downstairs to her brother and father, who were waiting at the hall door for her, the shoe dropped off; she put it on again in a great hurry; but, as she was going across the hall, her father turned round.

"Why are you walking slipshod? no one must walk slipshod with me. Why, Rosamond," said he, looking at her shoes with disgust, "I thought that you were always neat. Go, I cannot take you with me."

Imprudent: unwise

85   Rosamond colored and retired. "Oh, mamma," said she, as she took off her hat, "how I wish that I had chosen the shoes! they would have been of so much more use to me than that jar: however, I am sure—no, not quite sure—but I hope I shall be wiser another time."

QUESTIONS

1. From the text of paragraphs 1-18, what can you infer about the characters?

2. In paragraph 17, the reader learns what the point of view is. Identify the point of view and analyze what impact it has on the meaning and tone.

3. Determine the meanings and connotations of paragraph 52. What do they show about the mother-daughter relationship?

4. Consider the author's word choices in her description of the shoemaker's shop as well as her choice to name him Mr. Sole. What are the connotations and how do they affect the meaning and tone?

5. What important lesson is the mother trying to teach in paragraph 42?

6. Closely examine the meanings and connotations of paragraphs 44 to 50. How do the word choices give us a fuller understanding of the family's status and the tactics of the mother's attempt to educate her daughter?

7. How does paragraph 54 expand Rosamond's education even more?

8. When Rosamond gets home, she immediately picks all of her flowers and brings them in while she awaits the delivery of the big jar. What does this scene tell us about her and her mother?

9. Why does the author repeat the words "dark," "disagreeable," and "black" in paragraph 65? What is the impact on the meaning and tone?

10. Why did the author choose purple as the central color in the story?

11. What is one logical inference from paragraph 74?

12. What are the connotations of paragraph 81?

13. What can be inferred based on Rosamond's father's refusal to take her on a sight-seeing trip and her reaction to his decision?

14. In the last line of the story, Rosamond says she is "not quite sure" that she will "be wiser another time." What does her statement imply about her?

15. What are the two main themes of this short story? Discuss how they intertwine to produce a complex narrative.

Stephen Crane

The Open Boat

INTRODUCTION

The Open Boat

This harrowing, suspenseful story of a shipwreck and its survivors' ordeal is based on reality: Stephen Crane was on *The Commodore*, a cargo ship headed for Cuba, when it sank on January 2, 1897. Crane, the captain, the cook, and the oiler left the ship safely in one of the ten-foot dinghies, but faced almost impossible odds against staying alive. In a newspaper account published soon afterward and available on several websites, Crane writes, "The history of life in an open boat for thirty hours would no doubt be instructive for the young…." The short story was a central part of his collected works called *The Open Boat and Other Tales of Adventure* (1898).

Stephen Crane

A painstaking craftsman and pioneer in Naturalism, Stephen Crane produced some of the most vivid, vibrant fiction ever created—especially in his masterpiece, *The Red Badge of Courage*, a Civil War novel published in 1895—but his life and career were very short. He was born on November 1, 1871, in Newark, New Jersey, the son of a Methodist minister, who encouraged his son to write. Later, he attended various colleges, but Crane was never an enthusiastic or highly successful student and dropped out of Syracuse University in 1891 to become a writer.

Crane had spent time hunting and camping in Sullivan County, New York, a rural area about a hundred miles northwest of New York City. While there, he wrote a series of short stories that were published in the *New York Tribune* in 1892, and he became a regular contributor to the newspaper. In the fall of that year, he moved to a rooming house in Manhattan and spent some time in the Bowery, a neighborhood in the southern part of New York City. Based on his experiences there, he wrote his first novel, *Maggie: A Girl of the Streets* (1893). He published it privately, and received a good critical notice from Howells, but sold few copies.

Crane continued to earn a small amount as a freelance writer for various New York publications. Pulling together recollections of his childhood conversations with Civil War veterans and his reading of a series of articles recalling the conflict's battles, he began writing *The Red Badge of Courage* in 1893. The novel was first published in serial form in several newspapers, and by the time it came out as a book in 1895, it had become well known and much anticipated. Although he published poetry, stories, and many newspaper articles, nothing would ever approach the enormous success and popularity of his most important work, which has never been out of print.

Crane's lifestyle and unconventional views did not go over well in the strict, religious, business-oriented American culture near the turn of the century. In 1897, he moved to England, where he socialized with such well-known writers as H. G. Wells and Joseph Conrad. He had developed tuberculosis during his travels, however, and died on June 5, 1900, while undergoing treatment in the Black Forest in Germany.

The Open Boat
Stephen Crane (1897)

A Tale Intended to be after the Fact:
Being the Experience of Four Men from the Sunk
Steamer Commodore.

I

NONE OF THEM KNEW the color of the sky. Their eyes glanced level, and were fastened upon the waves that swept toward them. These waves were of the hue of slate, save for the tops, which were of foaming white, and all of the men knew the colors of the sea. The horizon narrowed and widened, and dipped and rose, and at all times its edge was jagged with waves that seemed thrust up in points like rocks.

Many a man ought to have a bath-tub larger than the boat which here rode upon the sea. These waves were most wrongfully and **barbarously** abrupt and tall, and each froth-top was a problem in small boat navigation.

Barbarously: in an uncivilized way

The cook squatted in the bottom and looked with both eyes at the six inches of **gunwale** which separated him from the ocean. His sleeves were rolled over his fat forearms, and the two flaps of his unbuttoned vest dangled as he bent to bail out the boat. Often he said: "Gawd! That was a narrow clip." As he remarked it, he invariably gazed eastward over the broken sea.

Gunwale: the top edge of a boat's side

The oiler, steering with one of the two oars in the boat, sometimes raised himself suddenly to keep clear of water that swirled in over the stern. It was a thin little oar and it seemed often ready to snap.

5   The correspondent, pulling at the other oar, watched the waves and wondered why he was there.

The injured captain, lying in the **bow**, was at this time buried in that profound dejection and indifference which comes, temporarily at least, to even the bravest and most enduring when, willy nilly, the firm fails, the army loses, the ship goes

Bow: the front of a boat

down. The mind of the master of a vessel is rooted deep in the timbers of her, though he command for a day or a decade, and this captain had on him the stern impression of a scene in the grays of dawn of seven turned faces, and later a stump of a top-mast with a white ball on it that slashed to and fro at the waves, went low and lower, and down. Thereafter there was something strange in his voice. Although steady, it was deep with mourning, and of a quality beyond oration or tears.

"Keep 'er a little more south, Billie," said he.

" 'A little more south,' sir," said the oiler in the stern.

A seat in this boat was not unlike a seat upon a bucking bronco, and, by the same token, a bronco is not much smaller. The craft pranced and reared, and plunged like an animal. As each wave came, and she rose for it, she seemed like a horse making at a fence outrageously high. The manner of her scramble over these walls of water is a mystic thing, and, moreover, at the top of them were ordinarily these problems in white water, the foam racing down from the summit of each wave, requiring a new leap, and a leap from the air. Then, after scornfully bumping a crest, she would slide, and race, and splash down a long incline and arrive bobbing and nodding in front of the next menace.

10   A singular disadvantage of the sea lies in the fact that after successfully **surmounting** one wave you discover that there is another behind it just as important and just as nervously anxious to do something effective in the way of swamping boats. In a ten-foot **dinghy** one can get an idea of the resources of the sea in the line of waves that is not probable to the average experience, which is never at sea in a dinghy. As each salty wall of water approached, it shut all else from the view of the men in the boat, and it was not difficult to imagine that this particular wave was the final outburst of the ocean, the last effort of the grim water. There was a terrible grace in the move of the waves, and they came in silence, save for the snarling of the crests.

The oiler's name on Crane's actual boat, the *Commodore*, was William "Billy" Higgins.

Surmounting: rising above

Dinghy: a small boat

In the **wan** light, the faces of the men must have been gray. Their eyes must have glinted in strange ways as they gazed steadily **astern**. Viewed from a balcony, the whole thing would doubtlessly have been weirdly picturesque. But the men in the boat had no time to see it, and if they had had leisure there were other things to occupy their minds. The sun swung steadily up the sky, and they knew it was broad day because the color of the sea changed from slate to emerald-green, streaked with **amber** lights, and the foam was like tumbling snow. The process of the breaking day was unknown to them. They were aware only of this effect upon the color of the waves that rolled toward them.

Wan: pale

Astern: toward the back of a boat

Amber: a transparent yellowish brown color

In disjointed sentences the cook and the correspondent argued as to the difference between a life-saving station and a house of refuge. The cook had said: "There's a house of refuge just north of the Mosquito Inlet Light, and as soon as they see us, they'll come off in their boat and pick us up."

"As soon as who see us?" said the correspondent.

"The crew," said the cook.

15   "Houses of refuge don't have crews," said the correspondent. "As I understand them, they are only places where clothes and grub are stored for the benefit of shipwrecked people. They don't carry crews."

"Oh, yes, they do," said the cook.

"No, they don't," said the correspondent.

"Well, we're not there yet, anyhow," said the oiler, in the stern.

"Well," said the cook, "perhaps it's not a house of refuge that I'm thinking of as being near Mosquito Inlet Light. Perhaps it's a life-saving station."

20   "We're not there yet," said the oiler, in the stern.

II

AS THE BOAT bounced from the top of each wave, the wind tore through the hair of the hatless men, and as the craft plopped her stern down again the spray slashed past them. The crest of each of these waves was a hill, from the top of which the men surveyed, for a moment, a broad tumultuous expanse; shining and wind-riven. It was probably splendid. It was probably glorious, this play of the free sea, wild with lights of emerald and white and amber.

"Bully good thing it's an on-shore wind," said the cook. "If not, where would we be? Wouldn't have a show."

"That's right," said the correspondent.

The busy oiler nodded his assent.

5   Then the captain, in the bow, chuckled in a way that expressed humor, contempt, tragedy, all in one. "Do you think we've got much of a show, now, boys?" said he.

Whereupon the three were silent, save for a trifle of hemming and hawing. To express any particular optimism at this time they felt to be childish and stupid, but they all doubtless possessed this sense of the situation in their mind. A young man thinks doggedly at such times. On the other hand, the ethics of their condition was decidedly against any open suggestion of hopelessness. So they were silent.

"Oh, well," said the captain, soothing his children, "we'll get ashore all right."

But there was that in his tone which made them think, so the oiler quoth: "Yes! If this wind holds!"

The cook was bailing: "Yes! If we don't catch hell in the surf."

10   Canton flannel gulls flew near and far. Sometimes they sat down on the sea, near patches of brown sea-weed that rolled over the waves with a movement like carpets on line in a gale. The birds sat comfortably in groups, and they were envied by some in the dinghy, for the wrath of the sea was no more to them than it was to a **covey** of prairie chickens a thousand miles inland. Often they came very close and stared at the men with black bead-like eyes. At these times they were uncanny and sinister in their unblinking scrutiny, and the men hooted angrily at them, telling them to be gone. One came, and evidently decided to alight on the top of the captain's head. The bird flew parallel to the boat and did not circle, but made short sidelong

Covey: a small group of birds

jumps in the air in chicken-fashion. His black eyes were **wistfully** fixed upon the captain's head. "Ugly brute," said the oiler to the bird. "You look as if you were made with a jack-knife." The cook and the correspondent swore darkly at the creature. The captain naturally wished to knock it away with the end of the heavy painter, but he did not dare do it, because anything resembling an emphatic gesture would have capsized this freighted boat, and so with his open hand, the captain gently and carefully waved the gull away. After it had been discouraged from the pursuit the captain breathed easier on account of his hair, and others breathed easier because the bird struck their minds at this time as being somehow gruesome and ominous.

In the meantime the oiler and the correspondent rowed. And also they rowed.

They sat together in the same seat, and each rowed an oar. Then the oiler took both oars; then the correspondent took both oars; then the oiler; then the correspondent. They rowed and they rowed. The very ticklish part of the business was when the time came for the reclining one in the stern to take his turn at the oars. By the very last star of truth, it is easier to steal eggs from under a hen than it was to change seats in the dinghy. First the man in the stern slid his hand along the **thwart** and moved with care, as if he were of **Sevres**. Then the man in the rowing seat slid his hand along the other thwart. It was all done with the most extraordinary care. As the two sidled past each other, the whole party kept watchful eyes on the coming wave, and the captain cried: "Look out now! Steady there!"

The brown mats of sea-weed that appeared from time to time were like islands, bits of earth. They were travelling, apparently, neither one way nor the other. They were, to all intents stationary. They informed the men in the boat that it was making progress slowly toward the land.

The captain, rearing cautiously in the bow, after the dinghy soared on a great swell, said that he

Wistfully: in a nostalgic way; longingly

Thwart: a crosspiece in a boat that can be used as a seat by a rower

Sèvres: expensive French pottery
The man is moving as if he were made of expensive pottery from the town of Sèvres in France.

had seen the lighthouse at Mosquito Inlet. Presently the cook remarked that he had seen it. The correspondent was at the oars, then, and for some reason he too wished to look at the lighthouse, but his back was toward the far shore and the waves were important, and for some time he could not seize an opportunity to turn his head. But at last there came a wave more gentle than the others, and when at the crest of it he swiftly scoured the western horizon.

15   "See it?" said the captain.

"No," said the correspondent, slowly, "I didn't see anything."

"Look again," said the captain. He pointed. "It's exactly in that direction."

At the top of another wave, the correspondent did as he was bid, and this time his eyes chanced on a small still thing on the edge of the swaying horizon. It was precisely like the point of a pin. It took an anxious eye to find a lighthouse so tiny.

"Think we'll make it, captain?"

20   "If this wind holds and the boat don't swamp, we can't do much else," said the captain.

The little boat, lifted by each towering sea, and splashed viciously by the crests, made progress that in the absence of sea-weed was not apparent to those in her. She seemed just a wee thing wallowing, miraculously, top-up, at the mercy of five oceans. Occasionally, a great spread of water, like white flames, swarmed into her.

"Bail her, cook," said the captain, serenely.

"All right, captain," said the cheerful cook.

III

IT WOULD BE difficult to describe the subtle brotherhood of men that was here established on the seas. No one said that it was so. No one mentioned it. But it dwelt in the boat, and each man felt it warm him. They were a captain, an oiler, a cook, and a correspondent, and they were friends, friends in a more curiously iron-bound degree than may be common. The hurt captain, lying against the water-jar in the bow, spoke always in a low voice and calmly, but he could never command a more ready and swiftly obedient crew than the **motley** three of the dinghy. It was more than a mere recognition of what was best for the common safety. There was surely in it a quality that was personal and heartfelt. And after this devotion to the commander of the boat there was this comradeship that the correspondent, for instance, who had been taught to be cynical of men, knew even at the time was the best experience of his life. But no one said that it was so. No one mentioned it.

Motley: composed of dissimilar elements

"I wish we had a sail," remarked the captain. "We might try my overcoat on the end of an oar and give you two boys a chance to rest." So the cook and the correspondent held the mast and spread wide the overcoat. The oiler steered, and the little boat made good way with her new rig. Sometimes the oiler had to scull sharply to keep a sea from breaking into the boat, but otherwise sailing was a success.

Meanwhile the light-house had been growing slowly larger. It had now almost assumed color, and appeared like a little gray shadow on the sky. The man at the oars could not be prevented from turning his head rather often to try for a glimpse of this little gray shadow.

At last, from the top of each wave the men in the tossing boat could see land. Even as the light-house was an upright shadow on the sky, this land seemed but a long black shadow on the sea. It certainly was thinner than paper. "We must be about opposite New Smyrna," said the cook, who had coasted this shore often in schooners. "Captain, by the way, I believe they abandoned that life-saving station there about a year ago."

5 "Did they?" said the captain.

The wind slowly died away. The cook and the correspondent were not now obliged to slave in order to hold high the oar. But the waves continued their old impetuous swooping at the dinghy, and the little craft, no longer under way, struggled

Apropos: regarding; relevant

Foundering: sinking

Ingenuously: innocently

Diabolical: devilish

Aberrations: flukes, variances from the norm

woundily over them. The oiler or the correspondent took the oars again.

Shipwrecks are **apropos** of nothing. If men could only train for them and have them occur when the men had reached pink condition, there would be less drowning at sea. Of the four in the dinghy none had slept any time worth mentioning for two days and two nights previous to embarking in the dinghy, and in the excitement of clambering about the deck of a **foundering** ship they had also forgotten to eat heartily.

For these reasons, and for others, neither the oiler nor the correspondent was fond of rowing at this time. The correspondent wondered **ingenuously** how in the name of all that was sane could there be people who thought it amusing to row a boat. It was not an amusement; it was a **diabolical** punishment, and even a genius of mental **aberrations** could never conclude that it was anything but a horror to the muscles and a crime against the back. He mentioned to the boat in general how the amusement of rowing struck him, and the weary-faced oiler smiled in full sympathy. Previously to the foundering, by the way, the oiler had worked double-watch in the engine-room of the ship.

"Take her easy, now, boys," said the captain. "Don't spend yourselves. If we have to run a surf you'll need all your strength, because we'll sure have to swim for it. Take your time."

10 Slowly the land arose from the sea. From a black line it became a line of black and a line of white, trees, and sand. Finally, the captain said that he could make out a house on the shore. "That's the house of refuge, sure," said the cook. "They'll see us before long, and come out after us."

The distant light-house reared high. "The keeper ought to be able to make us out now, if he's looking through a glass," said the captain. "He'll notify the life-saving people."

"None of those other boats could have got ashore to give word of the wreck," said the oiler, in a low voice. "Else the life-boat would be out hunting us."

Slowly and beautifully the land loomed out of the sea. The wind came again. It had veered from the northeast to the southeast. Finally, a new sound struck the ears of the men in the boat. It was the low thunder of the surf on the shore. "We'll never be able to make the light-house now," said the captain. "Swing her head a little more north, Billie," said the captain.

" 'A little more north,' sir," said the oiler.

15   Whereupon the little boat turned her nose once more down the wind, and all but the oarsman watched the shore grow. Under the influence of this expansion doubt and **direful** apprehension was leaving the minds of the men. The management of the boat was still most absorbing, but it could not prevent a quiet cheerfulness. In an hour, perhaps, they would be ashore.

Direful: causing fear

Their back-bones had become thoroughly used to balancing in the boat and they now rode this wild colt of a dinghy like circus men. The correspondent thought that he had been drenched to the skin, but happening to feel in the top pocket of his coat, he found therein eight cigars. Four of them were soaked with sea-water; four were perfectly **scatheless**. After a search, somebody produced three dry matches, and thereupon the four **waifs impudently** rode in their little boat, and with an assurance of an impending rescue shining in their eyes, puffed at the big cigars and judged well and ill of all men. Everybody took a drink of water.

Scatheless: unharmed, without damage

Waifs: helpless individuals or children

Impudently: without regard for consequences

IV

"COOK," REMARKED THE captain, "there don't seem to be any signs of life about your house of refuge."

"No," replied the cook. "Funny they don't see us!"

A broad stretch of lowly coast lay before the eyes of the men. It was of low dunes topped with dark vegetation. The roar of the surf was plain, and sometimes they could see the white lip of a wave as it spun up the beach. A tiny house was blocked out black upon the sky. Southward, the slim lighthouse lifted its little gray length.

Tide, wind, and waves were swinging the dinghy northward. "Funny they don't see us," said the men.

5   The surf's roar was here dulled, but its tone was, nevertheless, thunderous and mighty. As the boat swam over the great rollers, the men sat listening to this roar. "We'll swamp sure," said everybody.

It is fair to say here that there was not a life-saving station within twenty miles in either direction, but the men did not know this fact and in consequence they made dark and **opprobrious** remarks concerning the eyesight of the nation's life-savers. Four scowling men sat in the dinghy and surpassed records in the invention of **epithets**.

"Funny they don't see us."

The light-heartedness of a former time had completely faded. To their sharpened minds it was easy to **conjure** pictures of all kinds of incompetency and blindness and indeed, cowardice. There was the shore of the populous land, and it was bitter and bitter to them that from it came no sign.

"Well," said the captain, ultimately, "I suppose we'll have to make a try for ourselves. If we stay out here too long, we'll none of us have strength left to swim after the boat swamps."

10   And so the oiler, who was at the oars, turned the boat straight for the shore. There was a sudden tightening of muscles. There was some thinking.

"If we don't all get ashore—" said the captain. "If we don't all get ashore, I suppose you fellows know where to send news of my finish?"

They then briefly exchanged some addresses and **admonitions**. As for the reflections of the men, there was a great deal of rage in them. Perchance they might be formulated thus: "If I am going to be drowned—if I am going to be drowned—if I am going to be drowned, why, in the name of the seven mad gods who rule the sea, was I allowed to

Opprobrious: scornful and judgmental

Epithets: curses

Conjure: to make up, invent

Admonitions: words of caution

come thus far and contemplate sand and trees? Was I brought here merely to have my nose dragged away as I was about to nibble the sacred cheese of life? It is preposterous. If this old ninny-woman, Fate, cannot do better than this, she should be deprived of the management of men's fortunes. She is an old hen who knows not her intention. If she has decided to drown me, why did she not do it in the beginning and save me all this trouble. The whole affair is absurd…But, no, she cannot mean to drown me. She dare not drown me. She cannot drown me. Not after all this work." Afterward the man might have had an impulse to shake his fist at the clouds: "Just you drown me, now, and then hear what I call you!"

The **billows** that came at this time were more formidable. They seemed always just about to break and roll over the little boat in a turmoil of foam. There was a preparatory and long growl in the speech of them. No mind unused to the sea would have concluded that the dinghy could ascend these sheer heights in time. The shore was still afar. The oiler was a **wily** surfman. "Boys," he said, swiftly, "she won't live three minutes more and we're too far out to swim. Shall I take her to sea again, captain?"

Billows: large waves

Wily: cunning

"Yes! Go ahead!" said the captain.

15   This oiler, by a series of quick miracles, and fast and steady oarsmanship, turned the boat in the middle of the surf and took her safely to sea again.

There was a considerable silence as the boat bumped over the furrowed sea to deeper water. Then somebody in gloom spoke. "Well, anyhow, they must have seen us from the shore by now."

The gulls went in slanting flight up the wind toward the gray desolate east. A **squall**, marked by dingy clouds, and clouds brick-red, like smoke from a burning building, appeared from the southeast.

Squall: a burst of rain and wind

"What do you think of those life-saving people? Ain't they peaches?"

"Funny they haven't seen us."

20   "Maybe they think we're out here for sport! Maybe they think we're fishin'. Maybe they think we're damned fools."

It was a long afternoon. A changed tide tried to force them southward, but wind and wave said northward. Far ahead, where coast-line, sea, and sky formed their mighty angle, there were little dots which seemed to indicate a city on the shore.

"St. Augustine?"

The captain shook his head. "Too near Mosquito Inlet."

And the oiler rowed, and then the correspondent rowed. Then the oiler rowed. It was a weary business. The human back can become the seat of more aches and pains than are registered in books for the composite anatomy of a regiment. It is a limited area, but it can become the theatre of innumerable muscular conflicts, tangles, wrenches, knots, and other comforts.

25   "Did you ever like to row, Billie?" asked the correspondent.

"No," said the oiler. "Hang it."

When one exchanged the rowing-seat for a place in the bottom of the boat, he suffered a bodily depression that caused him to be careless of everything save an obligation to wiggle one finger. There was cold sea-water swashing to and fro in the boat, and he lay in it. His head, pillowed on a thwart, was within an inch of the swirl of a wave crest, and sometimes a particularly **obstreperous** sea came in-board and drenched him once more. But these matters did not annoy him. It is almost certain that if the boat had capsized he would have tumbled comfortably out upon the ocean as if he felt sure it was a great soft mattress.

Obstreperous: loud and unruly

"Look! There's a man on the shore!"

"Where?"

30   "There! See 'im? See 'im?"

"Yes, sure! He's walking along."

"Now he's stopped. Look! He's facing us!"

"He's waving at us!"

"So he is! By thunder!"

35   "Ah, now, we're all right! Now we're all right! There'll be a boat out here for us in half an hour."

"He's going on. He's running. He's going up to that house there."

The remote beach seemed lower than the sea, and it required a searching glance to discern the little black figure. The captain saw a floating stick and they rowed to it. A bath-towel was by some weird chance in the boat, and, tying this on the stick, the captain waved it. The oarsman did not dare turn his head, so he was obliged to ask questions.

"What's he doing now?"

"He's standing still again. He's looking, I think…There he goes again. Toward the house… Now he's stopped again."

40   "Is he waving at us?"

"No, not now! he was, though."

"Look! There comes another man!"

"He's running."

"Look at him go, would you."

45   "Why, he's on a bicycle. Now he's met the other man. They're both waving at us. Look!"

"There comes something up the beach."

"What the devil is that thing?"

"Why, it looks like a boat."

"Why, certainly it's a boat."

50   "No, it's on wheels."

"Yes, so it is. Well, that must be the life-boat. They drag them along shore on a wagon."

"That's the life-boat, sure."

"No, by—, it's—it's an **omnibus**."

"I tell you it's a life-boat."

55   "It is not! It's an omnibus. I can see it plain. See? One of these big hotel omnibuses."

Omnibus: a bus; a vehicle big enough for a large number of passengers

"By thunder, you're right. It's an omnibus, sure as fate. What do you suppose they are doing with an omnibus? Maybe they are going around collecting the life-crew, hey?"

"That's it, likely. Look! There's a fellow waving a little black flag. He's standing on the steps of the omnibus.

There come those other two fellows. Now they're all talking together. Look at the fellow with the flag. Maybe he ain't waving it."

"That ain't a flag, is it? That's his coat. Why, certainly, that's his coat."

60   "So it is. It's his coat. He's taken it off and is waving it around his head. But would you look at him swing it."

"Oh, say, there isn't any life-saving station there. That's just a winter resort hotel omnibus that has brought over some of the boarders to see us drown."

"What's that idiot with the coat mean? What's he signaling, anyhow?"

"It looks as if he were trying to tell us to go north. There must be a life-saving station up there."

"No! He thinks we're fishing. Just giving us a merry hand. See? Ah, there, Willie."

65   "Well, I wish I could make something out of those signals. What do you suppose he means?"

"He don't mean anything. He's just playing."

"Well, if he'd just signal us to try the surf again, or to go to sea and wait, or go north, or go south, or go to hell—there would be some reason in it. But look at him. He just stands there and keeps his coat revolving like a wheel. The ass!"

"There come more people."

"Now there's quite a mob. Look! Isn't that a boat?"

70   "Where? Oh, I see where you mean. No, that's no boat."

"That fellow is still waving his coat."

"He must think we like to see him do that. Why don't he quit it? It don't mean anything."

"I don't know. I think he is trying to make us go north. It must be that there's a life-saving station there somewhere."

"Say, he ain't tired yet. Look at 'im wave."

75   "Wonder how long he can keep that up. He's been revolving his coat ever since he caught sight of us. He's an idiot. Why aren't they getting men to bring a boat out. A fishing boat—one of those big **yawls**—could come out here all right. Why don't he do something?"

"Oh, it's all right, now."

"They'll have a boat out here for us in less than no time, now that they've seen us."

Yawls: sailboats with two masts

A faint yellow tone came into the sky over the low land. The shadows on the sea slowly deepened. The wind bore coldness with it, and the men began to shiver.

"Holy smoke!" said one, allowing his voice to express his impious mood, "if we keep on monkeying out here! If we've got to flounder out here all night!"

80 "Oh, we'll never have to stay here all night! Don't you worry. They've seen us now, and it won't be long before they'll come chasing out after us."

The shore grew dusky. The man waving a coat blended gradually into this gloom, and it swallowed in the same manner the omnibus and the group of people. The spray, when it dashed uproariously over the side, made the voyagers shrink and swear like men who were being branded.

"I'd like to catch the chump who waved the coat. I feel like soaking him one, just for luck."

"Why? What did he do?"

"Oh, nothing, but then he seemed so damned cheerful."

85 In the meantime the oiler rowed, and then the correspondent rowed, and then the oiler rowed. Gray-faced and bowed forward, they mechanically, turn by turn, plied the leaden oars. The form of the light-house had vanished from the southern horizon, but finally a pale star appeared, just lifting from the sea. The streaked saffron in the west passed before the all-merging darkness, and the sea to the east was black. The land had vanished, and was expressed only by the low and drear thunder of the surf.

"If I am going to be drowned—if I am going to be drowned—if I am going to be drowned, why, in the name of the seven mad gods, who rule the sea, was I allowed to come thus far and contemplate sand and trees? Was I brought here merely to have my nose dragged away as I was about to nibble the sacred cheese of life?"

The patient captain, drooped over the water-jar, was sometimes obliged to speak to the oarsman.

"Keep her head up! Keep her head up!"

" 'Keep her head up,' sir." The voices were weary and low.

90   This was surely a quiet evening. All save the oarsman lay heavily and listlessly in the boat's bottom. As for him, his eyes were just capable of noting the tall black waves that swept forward in a most sinister silence, save for an occasional subdued growl of a crest.

The cook's head was on a thwart, and he looked without interest at the water under his nose. He was deep in other scenes. Finally he spoke. "Billie," he murmured, dreamfully, "what kind of pie do you like best?"

V

"PIE," SAID THE OILER and the correspondent, agitatedly. "Don't talk about those things, blast you!"

"Well," said the cook, "I was just thinking about ham sandwiches, and—"

A night on the sea in an open boat is a long night. As darkness settled finally, the shine of the light, lifting from the sea in the south, changed to full gold. On the northern horizon a new light appeared, a small bluish gleam on the edge of the waters. These two lights were the furniture of the world. Otherwise there was nothing but waves.

Two men huddled in the stern, and distances were so magnificent in the dinghy that the rower was enabled to keep his feet partly warmed by thrusting them under his companions. Their legs indeed extended far under the rowing-seat until they touched the feet of the captain forward. Sometimes, despite the efforts of the tired oarsman, a wave came piling into the boat, an icy wave of the night, and the chilling water soaked them anew. They would twist their bodies for a moment and groan, and sleep the dead sleep once more, while the water in the boat gurgled about them as the craft rocked.

5   The plan of the oiler and the correspondent was for one to row until he lost the ability, and then arouse the other from his sea-water couch in the bottom of the boat.

The oiler plied the oars until his head drooped forward, and the overpowering sleep blinded him. And he rowed yet afterward. Then he touched a man in the bottom of the boat, and called his name. "Will you spell me for a little while?" he said, meekly.

"Sure, Billie," said the correspondent, awakening and dragging himself to a sitting position. They exchanged places carefully, and the oiler, cuddling down to the sea-water at the cook's side, seemed to go to sleep instantly.

The particular violence of the sea had ceased. The waves came without snarling. The obligation of the man at the oars was to keep the boat headed so that the tilt of the rollers would not capsize her, and to preserve her from filling when the crests rushed past. The black waves were silent and hard to be seen in the darkness. Often one was almost upon the boat before the oarsman was aware.

In a low voice the correspondent addressed the captain. He was not sure that the captain was awake, although this iron man seemed to be always awake. "Captain, shall I keep her making for that light north, sir?"

10   The same steady voice answered him. "Yes. Keep it about two points off the port bow."

The cook had tied a life-belt around himself in order to get even the warmth which this clumsy cork **contrivance** could donate, and he seemed almost stove-like when a rower, whose teeth invariably chattered wildly as soon as he ceased his labor, dropped down to sleep.

Contrivance: an invented object

The correspondent, as he rowed, looked down at the two men sleeping under foot. The cook's arm was around the oiler's shoulders, and, with their fragmentary clothing and haggard faces, they were the babes of the sea, a grotesque rendering of the old babes in the wood.

Later he must have grown stupid at his work, for suddenly there was a growling of water, and a crest came with a roar and a swash into the boat, and it was a wonder that it did not set the cook afloat in his life-belt. The cook continued to sleep, but the oiler sat up, blinking his eyes and shaking with the new cold.

"Oh, I'm awful sorry, Billie," said the correspondent, contritely.

15   "That's all right, old boy," said the oiler, and lay down again and was asleep.

Presently it seemed that even the captain dozed, and the correspondent thought that he was the one man afloat on all the oceans. The wind had a voice as it came over the waves, and it was sadder than the end.

Phosphorescence: a glow

There was a long, loud swishing astern of the boat, and a gleaming trail of **phosphorescence**, like blue flame, was furrowed on the black waters. It might have been made by a monstrous knife.

Then there came a stillness, while the correspondent breathed with the open mouth and looked at the sea.

Suddenly there was another swish and another long flash of bluish light, and this time it was alongside the boat, and might almost have been reached with an oar. The correspondent saw an enormous fin speed like a shadow through the water, hurling the crystalline spray and leaving the long glowing trail.

20   The correspondent looked over his shoulder at the captain. His face was hidden, and he seemed to be asleep. He looked at the babes of the sea. They certainly were asleep. So, being bereft of sympathy, he leaned a little way to one side and swore softly into the sea.

But the thing did not then leave the vicinity of the boat. Ahead or astern, on one side or the other, at intervals long or short, fled the long sparkling streak, and there was to be heard the whiroo of the dark fin. The speed and power of the thing was greatly to be admired. It cut the water like a gigantic and keen projectile.

The presence of this biding thing did not affect the man with the same horror that it would if he had been a picnicker. He simply looked at the sea dully and swore in an undertone.

Nevertheless, it is true that he did not wish to be alone with the thing. He wished one of his companions to awaken by chance and keep him company with it. But the captain hung motionless over the water-jar and the oiler and the cook in the bottom of the boat were plunged in slumber.

VI

"IF I AM going to be drowned—if I am going to be drowned—if I am going to be drowned, why, in the name of the seven mad gods, who rule the sea, was I allowed to come thus far and contemplate sand and trees?"

During this dismal night, it may be remarked that a man would conclude that it was really the intention of the seven mad gods to drown him, despite the abominable injustice of it. For it was certainly an abominable injustice to drown a man who had worked so hard, so hard. The man felt it would be a crime most unnatural. Other people had drowned at sea since galleys swarmed with painted sails, but still—

When it occurs to a man that nature does not regard him as important, and that she feels she would not maim the universe by disposing of him, he at first wishes to throw bricks at the temple, and he hates deeply the fact that there are no bricks and no temples. Any visible expression of nature would surely be pelleted with his jeers.

Then, if there be no tangible thing to hoot he feels, perhaps, the desire to confront a personification and indulge in pleas, bowed to one knee, and with hands **supplicant**, saying: "Yes, but I love myself."

5   A high cold star on a winter's night is the word he feels that she says to him. Thereafter he knows the **pathos** of his situation.

The men in the dinghy had not discussed these matters, but each had, no doubt, reflected upon them in silence and according to his mind. There was seldom any expression upon their faces save the general one of complete weariness. Speech was devoted to the business of the boat.

Supplicant: one who begs or pleads

Pathos: sadness; the quality of evoking pity

To chime the notes of his emotion, a verse mysteriously entered the correspondent's head. He had even forgotten that he had forgotten this verse, but it suddenly was in his mind.

> A soldier of the Legion lay dying in Algiers,
> There was lack of woman's nursing, there was dearth of woman's tears;
> But a comrade stood beside him, and he took that comrade's hand
> And he said: "I shall never see my own, my native land."

In his childhood, the correspondent had been made acquainted with the fact that a soldier of the Legion lay dying in Algiers, but he had never regarded the fact as important. **Myriads** of his school-fellows had informed him of the soldier's plight, but the dinning had naturally ended by making him perfectly indifferent. He had never considered it his affair that a soldier of the Legion lay dying in Algiers, nor had it appeared to him as a matter for sorrow. It was less to him than breaking of a pencil's point.

Myriads: large numbers

10   Now, however, it quaintly came to him as a human, living thing. It was no longer merely a picture of a few throes in the breast of a poet, meanwhile drinking tea and warming his feet at the grate; it was an actuality—stern, mournful, and fine.

The correspondent plainly saw the soldier. He lay on the sand with his feet out straight and still. While his pale left hand was upon his chest in an attempt to **thwart** the going of his life, the blood came between his fingers. In the far Algerian distance, a city of low square forms was set against a sky that was faint with the last sunset hues. The correspondent, plying the oars and dreaming of the slow and slower movements of the lips of the soldier, was moved by a profound and perfectly impersonal comprehension. He was sorry for the soldier of the Legion who lay dying in Algiers.

Thwart: to prevent

The thing which had followed the boat and waited had evidently grown bored at the delay. There was no longer to be heard the slash of the cut-water, and there was no longer the flame of the long trail. The light in the north still glimmered, but it was apparently no nearer to the boat. Sometimes the boom of the surf rang in the correspondent's ears, and he turned the craft seaward then and rowed harder. Southward, someone had evidently built a watch-fire on the beach. It was too low and too far to be seen, but it made a shimmering, **roseate** reflection upon the bluff back of it, and this could be discerned from the boat. The wind came stronger, and sometimes a wave suddenly raged out like a mountain-cat and there was to be seen the sheen and sparkle of a broken crest.

Roseate: having a rose-like color

The captain, in the bow, moved on his water-jar and sat erect. "Pretty long night," he observed to the correspondent. He looked at the shore. "Those life-saving people take their time."

"Did you see that shark playing around?"

15   "Yes, I saw him. He was a big fellow, all right."

"Wish I had known you were awake."

Later the correspondent spoke into the bottom of the boat.

"Billie!" There was a slow and gradual disentanglement. "Billie, will you spell me?"

"Sure," said the oiler.

20   As soon as the correspondent touched the cold comfortable sea-water in the bottom of the boat, and had huddled close to the cook's life-belt he was deep in sleep, despite the fact that his teeth played all the popular airs. This sleep was so good to him that it was but a moment before he heard a voice call his name in a tone that demonstrated the last stages of exhaustion. "Will you spell me?"

"Sure, Billie."

The light in the north had mysteriously vanished, but the correspondent took his course from the wide-awake captain.

Later in the night they took the boat farther out to sea, and the captain directed the cook to take one oar at the stern and keep the boat facing the seas. He was to call out if he should hear the thunder of the surf. This plan enabled the oiler and

Respite: a brief rest

Bequeathed: willed to, passed down

Carmine: red

the correspondent to get **respite** together. "We'll give those boys a chance to get into shape again," said the captain. They curled down and, after a few preliminary chatterings and trembles, slept once more the dead sleep. Neither knew they had **bequeathed** to the cook the company of another shark, or perhaps the same shark.

As the boat caroused on the waves, spray occasionally bumped over the side and gave them a fresh soaking, but this had no power to break their repose. The ominous slash of the wind and the water affected them as it would have affected mummies.

25   "Boys," said the cook, with the notes of every reluctance in his voice, "she's drifted in pretty close. I guess one of you had better take her to sea again." The correspondent, aroused, heard the crash of the toppled crests.

As he was rowing, the captain gave him some whiskey and water, and this steadied the chills out of him. "If I ever get ashore and anybody shows me even a photograph of an oar—"

At last there was a short conversation.

"Billie…Billie, will you spell me?"

"Sure," said the oiler.

VII

WHEN THE CORRESPONDENT again opened his eyes, the sea and the sky were each of the gray hue of the dawning. Later, **carmine** and gold was painted upon the waters. The morning appeared finally, in its splendor with a sky of pure blue, and the sunlight flamed on the tips of the waves.

On the distant dunes were set many little black cottages, and a tall white wind-mill reared above them. No man, nor dog, nor bicycle appeared on the beach. The cottages might have formed a deserted village.

The voyagers scanned the shore. A conference was held in the boat. "Well," said the captain, "if no help is coming, we might better try a run through the surf right away. If we stay out here much longer we will be too weak to do anything for ourselves at all." The others silently **acquiesced** in this reasoning. The boat was headed for the beach. The correspondent wondered if none ever ascended the tall wind-tower, and if then they never looked seaward. This tower was a giant, standing with its back to the plight of the ants. It represented in a degree, to the correspondent, the serenity of nature amid the struggles of the individual—nature in the wind, and nature in the vision of men. She did not seem cruel to him, nor beneficent, nor treacherous, nor wise. But she was indifferent, flatly indifferent. It is, perhaps, plausible that a man in this situation, impressed with the unconcern of the universe, should see the innumerable flaws of his life and have them taste wickedly in his mind and wish for another chance. A distinction between right and wrong seems absurdly clear to him, then, in this new ignorance of the grave-edge, and he understands that if he were given another opportunity he would mend his conduct and his words, and be better and brighter during an introduction, or at a tea.

> **Acquiesced**: gave in, accepted

"Now, boys," said the captain, "she is going to swamp sure. All we can do is to work her in as far as possible, and then when she swamps, pile out and scramble for the beach. Keep cool now and don't jump until she swamps sure."

5   The oiler took the oars. Over his shoulders he scanned the surf. "Captain," he said, "I think I'd better bring her about, and keep her head-on to the seas and back her in."

"All right, Billie," said the captain. "Back her in." The oiler swung the boat then and, seated in the stern, the cook and the correspondent were obliged to look over their shoulders to contemplate the lonely and indifferent shore.

The monstrous inshore rollers heaved the boat high until the men were again enabled to see the white sheets of water scudding up the slanted beach. "We won't get in very close," said the captain. Each time a man could wrest his attention from the rollers, he turned his glance toward the shore, and in the expression of the eyes during this contemplation there was a singular quality. The correspondent, observing the others, knew that they were not afraid, but the full meaning of their glances was shrouded.

As for himself, he was too tired to grapple fundamentally with the fact. He tried to coerce his mind into thinking of it, but the mind was dominated at this time by the muscles, and the muscles said they did not care. It merely occurred to him that if he should drown it would be a shame.

Pallor: paleness

There were no hurried words, no **pallor**, no plain agitation. The men simply looked at the shore. "Now, remember to get well clear of the boat when you jump," said the captain.

10   Seaward the crest of a roller suddenly fell with a thunderous crash, and the long white **comber** came roaring down upon the boat.

Comber: a curving wave

"Steady now," said the captain. The men were silent. They turned their eyes from the shore to the comber and waited. The boat slid up the incline, leaped at the furious top, bounced over it, and swung down the long back of the waves. Some water had been shipped and the cook bailed it out.

But the next crest crashed also. The tumbling boiling flood of white water caught the boat and whirled it almost perpendicular. Water swarmed in from all sides. The correspondent had his hands on the gunwale at this time, and when the water entered at that place he swiftly withdrew his fingers, as if he objected to wetting them.

The little boat, drunken with this weight of water, reeled and snuggled deeper into the sea.

"Bail her out, cook! Bail her out," said the captain.

15   "All right, captain," said the cook.

"Now, boys, the next one will do for us, sure," said the oiler. "Mind to jump clear of the boat."

The third wave moved forward, huge, furious, **implacable**. It fairly swallowed the dinghy, and almost simultaneously the men tumbled into the sea. A piece of life-belt had lain in the bottom of the

Implacable: uncaring, incapable of being appeased

boat, and as the correspondent went overboard he held this to his chest with his left hand.

The January water was icy, and he reflected immediately that it was colder than he had expected to find it off the coast of Florida. This appeared to his dazed mind as a fact important enough to be noted at the time. The coldness of the water was sad; it was tragic. This fact was somehow mixed and confused with his opinion of his own situation that it seemed almost a proper reason for tears. The water was cold.

When he came to the surface he was conscious of little but the noisy water. Afterward he saw his companions in the sea. The oiler was ahead in the race. He was swimming strongly and rapidly. Off to the correspondent's left, the cook's great white and corked back bulged out of the water, and in the rear the captain was hanging with his one good hand to the **keel** of the overturned dinghy.

Keel: the bottom of a boat

20   There is a certain immovable quality to a shore, and the correspondent wondered at it amid the confusion of the sea.

It seemed also very attractive, but the correspondent knew that it was a long journey, and he paddled leisurely. The piece of life-preserver lay under him, and sometimes he whirled down the incline of a wave as if he were on a hand-sled.

But finally he arrived at a place in the sea where travel was beset with difficulty. He did not pause swimming to inquire what manner of current had caught him, but there his progress ceased. The shore was set before him like a bit of scenery on a stage, and he looked at it and understood with his eyes each detail of it.

As the cook passed, much farther to the left, the captain was calling to him, "Turn over on your back, cook! Turn over on your back and use the oar."

"All right, sir!" The cook turned on his back, and, paddling with an oar, went ahead as if he were a canoe.

25   Presently the boat also passed to the left of the correspondent with the captain clinging with one hand to the keel. He would have appeared like a man raising himself to look over a board fence, if it were not for the extraordinary gymnastics of the boat. The correspondent marveled that the captain could still hold to it.

They passed on, nearer to shore—the oiler, the cook, the captain—and following them went the water-jar, bouncing gayly over the seas.

The correspondent remained in the grip of this strange new enemy—a current. The shore, with its white slope of sand and its green bluff, topped with little silent cottages, was spread like a picture before him. It was very near to him then, but he was impressed as one who in a gallery looks at a scene from Brittany or Algiers.

He thought: "I am going to drown? Can it be possible? Can it be possible? Can it be possible?" Perhaps an individual must consider his own death to be the final phenomenon of nature.

But later a wave perhaps whirled him out of this small deadly current, for he found suddenly that he could again make progress toward the shore. Later still, he was aware that the captain, clinging with one hand to the keel of the dinghy, had his face turned away from the shore and toward him, and was calling his name. "Come to the boat! Come to the boat!"

30   In his struggle to reach the captain and the boat, he reflected that when one gets properly wearied, drowning must really be a comfortable arrangement, a **cessation** of hostilities accompanied by a large degree of relief, and he was glad of it, for the main thing in his mind for some moments had been horror of the temporary agony. He did not wish to be hurt.

Presently he saw a man running along the shore. He was undressing with most remarkable speed. Coat, trousers, shirt, everything flew magically off him.

"Come to the boat," called the captain.

Cessation: a stoppage

"All right, captain." As the correspondent paddled, he saw the captain let himself down to bottom and leave the boat. Then the correspondent performed his one little marvel of the voyage. A large wave caught him and flung him with ease and supreme speed completely over the boat and far beyond it. It struck him even then as an event in gymnastics, and a true miracle of the sea. An overturned boat in the surf is not a plaything to a swimming man.

The correspondent arrived in water that reached only to his waist, but his condition did not enable him to stand for more than a moment. Each wave knocked him into a heap, and the under-tow pulled at him.

35   Then he saw the man who had been running and undressing, and undressing and running, come bounding into the water. He dragged ashore the cook, and then waded toward the captain, but the captain waved him away, and sent him to the correspondent. He was naked, naked as a tree in winter, but a halo was about his head, and he shone like a saint. He gave a strong pull, and a long drag, and a bully heave at the correspondent's hand. The correspondent, schooled in the minor formulae, said: "Thanks, old man." But suddenly the man cried: "What's that?" He pointed a swift finger. The correspondent said: "Go."

In the shallows, face downward, lay the oiler. His forehead touched sand that was periodically, between each wave, clear of the sea.

The correspondent did not know all that transpired afterward. When he achieved safe ground he fell, striking the sand with each particular part of his body. It was as if he had dropped from a roof, but the thud was grateful to him.

It seems that instantly the beach was populated with men with blankets, clothes, and flasks, and women with coffee-pots and all the remedies sacred to their minds. The welcome of the land to the men from the sea was warm and generous, but a still and dripping shape was carried slowly up the beach, and the land's welcome for it could only be the different and sinister hospitality of the grave.

When it came night, the white waves paced to and fro in the moonlight, and the wind brought the sound of the great sea's voice to the men on shore, and they felt that they could then be interpreters.

QUESTIONS

1. How does the author's choice to name only one of the characters contribute to the story's meaning and impact?

2. Analyze the effects of the following sentences that describe the perils of the boat and its passengers: "A seat in this boat was not unlike a seat upon a bucking bronco....The craft pranced and reared and plunged like an animal....Then, after scornfully bumping a crest, she would slide and race and splash down a long incline and arrive bobbing and nodding in front of the next menace" (part I, paragraph 9).

3. In part II, the captain says he sees a distant lighthouse. What meanings and inferences can be drawn from the following passage: "The correspondent was at the oars, then, and for some reason he too wished to look at the lighthouse...." At first, he fails to see it. Then, "his eyes chanced on a small, still thing...precisely like the point of a pin. It took an anxious eye to find a lighthouse so tiny." What does the author leave us uncertain about? Why?

4. What are the denotations and connotations of the narrator's depiction of the seagulls just after the beginning of part II? What do these irritating birds "with black bead-like eyes" symbolize?

5. The author specifically introduces the idea of the "brotherhood of men" in part III, paragraph 1. How and why does the point of view change throughout the paragraph? What is able to be logically inferred from the thoughts of the correspondent?

6. At the end of part III, the tone is lightened by this passage: "the four waifs rode impudently in their little boat, and, with an assurance of an impending rescue shining in their eyes, puffed at the big cigars...." What are the connotations of the author's word choices here and how does the background of uncertainty shade the meanings of the words?

7. In part IV, paragraph 12, Fate is introduced as both a force and a character toward which the men feel "a great deal of rage." Determine the explicit meaning and implications of this sentence: "Was I brought here merely to have my nose dragged away as I was about to nibble the sacred cheese of life?"

8. In part V, the men are so exhausted they fall asleep as soon as they get to lie down in the boat. List at least three examples of Crane's distinctive imagery and explain how his descriptions strengthen the theme of brotherhood.

9. How is the nightmarish impact of the correspondent's encounter with the shark made more powerful by the figurative and connotative meanings of the author's word choices? Cite specific examples.

10. Analyze how the concepts of "the brotherhood of man" and "man versus nature" build on one another, especially in part VI, paragraphs 2-5.

11. Beginning in part VI, paragraph 7, the correspondent recalls a well-known verse about a dying soldier (from "Bingen on the Rhine" by Caroline Norton). What can you infer based on the correspondent's new perspective regarding the soldier, and what is the literary term for this sudden change of heart?

12. What are some connotations of the imagery and the impact of the following passage on the tone of the short story: "This tower was a giant, standing with its back to the plight of the ants" (part VII, paragraph 3)?

13. Although the text explicitly tells of the men approaching the safety of the beach, cite at least three examples of word choices that are ominous, implying that the crew still faces uncertainty and danger.

14. In the last sentence, the text makes it clear that the men hear "the great sea's voice," but the story ends with a statement whose meaning is uncertain. What inferences can be made about the men feeling "that they could then be interpreters"?

15. Along with "brotherhood" and "man versus nature," "The Open Boat" also focuses on Fate. How does this motif work with the other two to add complexity to the story?

16. How does the structure of the story contribute to its overall impact?

17. The author often uses personification. List at least three examples and explain what they add to the effectiveness of "The Open Boat."

18. "The Open Boat" and "To Build a Fire" were both published close to 1900, and both are examples of Naturalism. In an objective essay, compare the stories by focusing on how they treat the "man versus nature" conflict.

19. What are three lessons that you can infer from the text of "The Open Boat"? In other words, what does the author want to teach us?

20. What is the main tone of "The Open Boat"? List an example of a word choice or brief passage from each of the seven parts that emphasizes and strengthens this overall mood.

Kate Chopin

The Story of an Hour

INTRODUCTION

The Story of an Hour

This deceptively simple depiction of a family tragedy was written on April 19, 1894. Having first appeared in *Vogue* in December of that same year as "The Dream of an Hour," it was reprinted in *St. Louis Life* magazine as "The Story of an Hour" on January 5, 1895. Slated for inclusion in a collection called *A Vocation and a Voice*, the story would not appear in a book by that name until 1991. In 1900, the collection was suddenly returned to her by the publisher, a decision that Chopin no doubt attributed to the controversy over her novel, *The Awakening* (1899). The second rejection that year, it further shattered Chopin's confidence. She would never again be a productive, enthusiastic writer.

Kate Chopin

Kate Chopin was relatively well known as a good short story writer during her lifetime, having published in major magazines such as *The Atlantic Monthly* and *The Century*, and collected her stories in two popular books, *Bayou Folk* (1894) and *A Night in Acadie* (1897). However, her two novels, *At Fault* (1890) and *The Awakening*, were not critical successes until years after her death. Her writings were rediscovered in the 1960s and 1970s. Chopin is now known as one of the most significant writers of the late nineteenth century and one of the strongest female voices in American literature.

Born on February 8, 1850, as Katherine O'Flaherty, Chopin was raised in her birth city of St. Louis, Missouri. Her father was Irish and her mother of French descent, and Kate grew up as a bilingual speaker. Later, she would translate some of the stories of Guy de Maupassant and try to duplicate his detailed, clever, surprising style in some of her own writing. At age five, she endured the first of several traumatic events in her life: Her father was killed when a railway bridge collapsed with him aboard the train. During the Civil War, Chopin also lost her great-grandmother; her half-brother, who was serving in the Confederate army, died of typhoid fever.

In 1868, she graduated from school and about a year later, met Oscar Chopin, a Louisiana native, who became her husband in 1870. The couple moved to New Orleans, where Oscar went into the cotton business. By 1879, they had six children, but Oscar caught malaria and died with large debts. Chopin finally settled his estate and returned to St. Louis in 1884 with her children, at first living with her mother, who passed away in 1885. Chopin had to figure out how to raise her children with virtually no help or steady income. Her doctor, a long-time family friend, told her that she might be able to write for a living, and soon she began a prolific literary career, writing and publishing nearly one hundred stories, along with her two novels.

However, after the hostility shown toward *The Awakening*, Chopin managed to publish only a few more stories, and at the age of 54, she died of a cerebral hemorrhage.

The Story of an Hour
Kate Chopin (1894)

KNOWING THAT MRS. MALLARD was afflicted with a heart trouble, great care was taken to break to her as gently as possible the news of her husband's death.

It was her sister Josephine who told her, in broken sentences; **veiled** hints that revealed in half concealing. Her husband's friend Richards was there, too, near her. It was he who had been in the newspaper office when intelligence of the railroad disaster was received, with Brently Mallard's name leading the list of "killed." He had only taken the time to assure himself of its truth by a second telegram, and had hastened to forestall any less careful, less tender friend in bearing the sad message.

Veiled: partially hidden

She did not hear the story as many women have heard the same, with a paralyzed inability to accept its significance. She wept at once, with sudden, wild abandonment, in her sister's arms. When the storm of grief had spent itself, she went away to her room alone. She would have no one follow her.

There stood, facing the open window, a comfortable, roomy armchair. Into this she sank, pressed down by a physical exhaustion that haunted her body and seemed to reach into her soul.

5   She could see in the open square before her house the tops of trees that were all **aquiver** with the new spring life. The delicious breath of rain was in the air. In the street below a peddler was crying his wares. The notes of a distant song which some one was singing reached her faintly, and countless sparrows were twittering in the eaves.

Aquiver: trembling, quivering

There were patches of blue sky showing here and there through the clouds that had met and piled one above the other in the west facing her window.

She sat with her head thrown back upon the cushion of the chair, quite motionless, except when a sob came up into her throat and shook her, as a child who has cried itself to sleep continues to sob in its dreams.

She was young, with a fair, calm face, whose lines bespoke **repression** and even a certain strength. But now there was a dull stare in her eyes, whose gaze was fixed away off yonder on one of those patches of blue sky. It was not a glance of reflection, but rather indicated a suspension of intelligent thought.

Repression: the state of being controlled or of holding back one's emotions

There was something coming to her and she was waiting for it, fearfully. What was it? She did not know; it was too subtle and elusive to name. But she felt it, creeping out of the sky, reaching toward her through the sounds, the scents, the color that filled the air.

10   Now her bosom rose and fell tumultuously. She was beginning to recognize this thing that was approaching to possess her, and she was striving to beat it back with her will—as powerless as her two white slender hands would have been. When she abandoned herself, a little whispered word escaped her slightly parted lips. She said it over and over under her breath: "free, free, free!" The vacant stare and the look of terror that had followed it went from her eyes. They stayed keen and bright. Her pulses beat fast, and the coursing blood warmed and relaxed every inch of her body.

She did not stop to ask if it were, or were not, a monstrous joy that held her. A clear and **exalted** perception enabled her to dismiss the suggestion as trivial.

Exalted: heightened

She knew that she would weep again when she saw the kind, tender hands folded in death; the face that had never looked save with love upon her, fixed and gray and dead. But she saw beyond that bitter moment a long procession of years to come that would belong to her absolutely. And she opened and spread her arms out to them in welcome.

There would be no one else to live for her during those coming years; she would live for herself. There would be no powerful will bending hers in that blind persistence with which men and women believe they have a right to impose upon a fellow-creature. A kind intention or a cruel intention made the act seem no less a crime as she looked upon it in that brief moment of illumination.

And yet she had loved him—sometimes. Often she had not. What did it matter! What could love, the unsolved mystery, count for in face of this possession of self-assertion which she suddenly recognized as the strongest impulse of her being!

15   "Free! Body and soul free!" she kept whispering.

Josephine was kneeling before the closed door with her lips to the keyhole, **imploring** for admission. "Louise, open the door! I beg; open the door—you will make yourself ill. What are you doing, Louise? For heaven's sake open the door."

Imploring: begging

"Go away. I am not making myself ill." No; she was drinking in a very **elixir** of life through that open window.

Elixir: a potion for the bettering of one's health

Her fancy was running riot along those days ahead of her. Spring days, and summer days, and all sorts of days that would be her own. She breathed a quick prayer that life might be long. It was only yesterday she had thought with a shudder, that life might be long.

She arose at length and opened the door to her sister's importunities. There was a feverish triumph in her eyes, and she carried herself unwittingly like a goddess of Victory. She clasped her sister's waist, and together they descended the stairs. Richards stood waiting for them at the bottom.

The winged "goddess of Victory" in Greek mythology was named Nike; the Romans called her Victoria.

20   Some one was opening the front door with a latchkey. It was Brently Mallard who entered, a little travel-stained, composedly carrying his grip-sack and umbrella. He had been far from the scene of accident, and did not even know there had been one. He stood amazed at Josephine's piercing cry; at Richards' quick motion to screen him from the view of his wife.

But Richards was too late.

When the doctors came, they said she had died of heart disease—of joy that kills.

QUESTIONS

1. Analyze paragraph 8. How does it characterize Mrs. Mallard and her marriage? What does the paragraph leave uncertain but hinted at?

2. Determine two important themes that develop over the course of "The Story of an Hour" and relate to Mrs. Mallard's mixed feelings for her husband.

3. Analyze how Kate Chopin blends these themes to make the story more complex and realistic. For example, specify at least two instances where the themes interact and build on one another.

4. Based on your understanding of the story, what actual meanings can a careful reader infer from the explicit text of the final sentence: "When the doctors came, they said she had died of heart disease—of joy that kills"?

5. Analyze how Chopin's presentation of Mrs. Mallard's point of view in the middle of "The Story of an Hour" strengthens the irony at the end.

6. What connotations and impact does the title have on the meaning of the story?

Jack London

To Build a Fire

INTRODUCTION

To Build a Fire

One of Jack London's famous tales of the Klondike Gold Rush in the 1890s, this intense story of a miner trying to survive in the coldest climate is a time-honored American classic. An expertly crafted example of Naturalism, it was first published in August 1908 in *The Century Magazine* and later included in London's collection called *Lost Face* (1910). An earlier version written for younger readers had appeared in *The Youth's Companion* in May 1902. This youth-oriented version is clearly more instructive than artistic, beginning, "For land travel or seafaring, the world over, a companion is usually considered desirable." Unlike the more popular and more realistic later version, there is no dog, the man has a name, and he does survive the cold.

Jack London

London enjoyed worldwide fame during the height of his writing career and for some years after his death. Beginning in the 1960s, his work began to receive new attention, acclaim, and serious study. He is now known as one of the most important Naturalist writers, and his major novels, *The Call of the Wild* (1903), *The Sea Wolf* (1904), *White Fang* (1906), and the autobiographical *Martin Eden* (1909), all of which have been made into movies, have carved out a permanent niche for him in American literature. He was also an influential journalist, environmentalist, and social activist.

Born in San Francisco as John Griffith Chaney on January 12, 1876, London was the son of an unwed mother. She eventually married John London, a veteran of the Civil War, who moved the family to Oakland. Restless for adventure and independence, Jack London left home at age 16 and worked at various jobs before discovering he had a love and a talent for sailing. In 1891, he bought his own boat and became an "oyster pirate," stealing from oyster beds around San Francisco. Soon after that, he served as a professional seaman, going to such places as Japan, Hawaii, and the Yukon. By 1896, he had joined the Socialist Labor Party and, in the fall, had enrolled at the University of California, where he stayed for only one semester. Meanwhile, he had already started writing, winning a writing contest in 1893, and his political letters were being regularly accepted by San Francisco newspapers.

"Two Gold Bricks," the first short story of London's to be published, appeared in September 1897, while London was prospecting in the Yukon. In 1898, he returned to Oakland, and decided to make his living as a writer. London managed to publish over 20 other works in 1899, including essays and poems, as well as stories. Financially, however, he was still struggling. In 1900, London published his first collection of fiction, *The Son of the Wolf*, followed three years later by his novel, *The Call of the Wild* (1903), which brought him great success and made him a world-famous author. London also wrote several plays.

In 1913, while undergoing an appendectomy, London was found to have kidney disease. Two years later, he traveled to Hawaii in hopes of improving his health. Despite London's health issues, however, he insisted on attending the California State Fair in September 1916. At his ranch in the Sonoma Valley, London became very ill in and on November 22, 1916, he died in his sleep, probably due to kidney failure.

To Build a Fire
Jack London (1908)

DAY HAD BROKEN cold and grey, exceedingly cold and grey, when the man turned aside from the main Yukon trail and climbed the high earth bank, where a dim and little-traveled trail led eastward through the fat spruce timberland. It was a steep bank, and he paused for breath at the top, excusing the act to himself by looking at his watch. It was nine o'clock. There was no sun nor hint of sun, though there was not a cloud in the sky. It was a clear day, and yet there seemed an **intangible pall** over the face of things, a subtle gloom that made the day dark, and that was due to the absence of sun. This fact did not worry the man. He was used to the lack of sun. It had been days since he had seen the sun, and he knew that a few more days must pass before that cheerful orb, due south, would just peep above the skyline and dip immediately from view.

The man flung a look back along the way he had come. The Yukon lay a mile wide and hidden under three feet of ice. On top of this ice were as many feet of snow. It was all pure white, rolling in gentle **undulations** where the ice jams of the freeze-up had formed. North and south, as far as his eye could see, it was unbroken white, save for a dark hairline that curved and twisted from around the spruce-covered island to the south, and that curved and twisted away into the north, where it disappeared behind another spruce-covered island. This dark hairline was the trail—the main trail—that led south five hundred miles to the Chilcoot Pass, Dyea, and salt water; and that led north seventy miles to Dawson, and still on to the north a thousand miles to Nulato, and finally to St. Michael on Bering Sea, a thousand miles and half a thousand more.

But all this—the mysterious, far-reaching hairline trail, the absence of sun from the sky, the tremendous cold, and the strangeness and weirdness of it all—made no impression on the man. It was

Intangible: unable to be touched or understood

Pall: a gloomy atmosphere

Undulations: wavelike motions

Dyea is a town in southeast Alaska that was a popular supply base for miners. The other places are stops along the route to the gold fields.

not because he was long used to it. He was a newcomer in the land, a Chechaquo, and this was his first winter. The trouble with him was that he was without imagination. He was quick and alert in the things of life, but only in the things, and not in their significances. Fifty degrees below zero meant eighty odd degrees of frost. Such a fact impressed him as being cold and uncomfortable, and that was all. It did not lead him to meditate upon his frailty as a creature of temperature, and upon man's frailty in general, able only to live within certain narrow limits of heat and cold; and from there on it did not lead him to the **conjectural** field of immortality and man's place in the universe. Fifty degrees below zero stood for a bite of frost that hurt and that must be guarded against by the use of mittens, earflaps, warm moccasins, and thick socks. Fifty degrees below zero was to him just precisely fifty degrees below zero. That there should be anything more to it than that was a thought that never entered his head.

As he turned to go on, he spat speculatively. There was a sharp, explosive crackle that startled him. He spat again. And again, in the air, before it could fall to the snow, the spittle crackled. He knew that at fifty below spittle crackled on the snow, but this spittle had crackled in the air. Undoubtedly it was colder than fifty below—how much colder he did not know. But the temperature did not matter. He was bound for the old claim on the left fork of Henderson Creek, where the boys were already. They had come over across the divide from the Indian Creek country, while he had come the roundabout way to take a look at the possibilities of getting out logs in the spring from the islands in the Yukon. He would be in to camp by six o'clock; a bit after dark, it was true, but the boys would be there, a fire would be going, and a hot supper would be ready. As for lunch, he pressed his hand against the protruding bundle under his jacket. It was also under his shirt, wrapped up in a handkerchief and lying against the naked skin. It was the only way to keep the biscuits from freezing. He smiled

"Chechaquo" means "newcomer" or "tenderfoot" in the Chinook language.

Conjectural: based on guesses and possibilities

agreeably to himself as he thought of those biscuits, each cut open and sopped in bacon grease, and each enclosing a generous slice of fried bacon.

5   He plunged in among the big spruce trees. The trail was faint. A foot of snow had fallen since the last sled had passed over, and he was glad he was without a sled, traveling light. In fact, he carried nothing but the lunch wrapped in the handkerchief. He was surprised, however, at the cold. It certainly was cold, he concluded, as he rubbed his numbed nose and cheekbones with his mittened hand. He was a warm-whiskered man, but the hair on his face did not protect the high cheekbones and the eager nose that thrust itself aggressively into the frosty air.

At the man's heels trotted a dog, a big native husky, the proper wolf-dog, grey-coated and without any visible or temperamental difference from its brother, the wild wolf. The animal was depressed by the tremendous cold. It knew that it was no time for traveling. Its instinct told it a truer tale than was told to the man by the man's judgment. In reality, it was not merely colder than fifty below zero; it was colder than sixty below, than seventy below. It was seventy-five below zero. Since the freezing-point is thirty-two above zero, it meant that one hundred and seven degrees of frost obtained. The dog did not know anything about thermometers. Possibly in its brain there was no sharp consciousness of a condition of very cold such as was in the man's brain. But the brute had its instinct. It experienced a vague but menacing apprehension that subdued it and made it slink along at the man's heels, and that made it question eagerly every **unwonted** movement of the man as if expecting him to go into camp or to seek shelter somewhere and build a fire. The dog had learned fire, and it wanted fire, or else to burrow under the snow and cuddle its warmth away from the air.

The frozen moisture of its breathing had settled on its fur in a fine powder of frost, and especially were its **jowls**, muzzle, and eyelashes whitened

Unwonted: unknown or unusual

Jowls: jaws

by its crystalled breath. The man's red beard and moustache were likewise frosted, but more solidly, the deposit taking the form of ice and increasing with every warm, moist breath he exhaled. Also, the man was chewing tobacco, and the muzzle of ice held his lips so rigidly that he was unable to clear his chin when he expelled the juice. The result was that a crystal beard of the colour and solidity of **amber** was increasing its length on his chin. If he fell down it would shatter itself, like glass, into brittle fragments. But he did not mind the **appendage**. It was the penalty all tobacco chewers paid in that country, and he had been out before in two cold snaps. They had not been so cold as this, he knew, but by the **spirit thermometer** at Sixty Mile he knew they had been registered at fifty below and at fifty-five.

He held on through the level stretch of woods for several miles, crossed a wide flat of niggerheads, and dropped down a bank to the frozen bed of a small stream. This was Henderson Creek, and he knew he was ten miles from the forks. He looked at his watch. It was ten o'clock. He was making four miles an hour, and he calculated that he would arrive at the forks at half-past twelve. He decided to celebrate that event by eating his lunch there.

The dog dropped in again at his heels, with a tail drooping discouragement, as the man swung along the creek bed. The **furrow** of the old sled trail was plainly visible, but a dozen inches of snow covered the marks of the last runners. In a month no man had come up or down that silent creek. The man held steadily on. He was not much given to thinking, and just then particularly he had nothing to think about save that he would eat lunch at the forks and that at six o'clock he would be in camp with the boys. There was nobody to talk to and, had there been, speech would have been impossible because of the ice-muzzle on his mouth. So he continued monotonously to chew tobacco and to increase the length of his amber beard.

Amber: a transparent yellowish brown color

Appendage: an attachment

Spirit thermometer: a thermometer that uses alcohol instead of mercury

Furrow: a groove

Pang: a severe pain

10   Once in a while, the thought reiterated itself that it was very cold and that he had never experienced such cold. As he walked along he rubbed his cheekbones and nose with the back of his mittened hand. He did this automatically, now and again changing hands. But rub as he would, the instant he stopped his cheekbones went numb, and the following instant, the end of his nose went numb. He was sure to frost his cheeks; he knew that and experienced a **pang** of regret that he had not devised a nose-strap of the sort Bud wore in cold snaps. Such a strap passed across the cheeks, as well, and saved them. But it didn't matter much, after all. What were frosted cheeks? A bit painful, that was all; they were never serious.

Empty as the man's mind was of thoughts, he was keenly observant, and he noticed the changes in the creek, the curves and bends and timber jams, and always he sharply noted where he placed his feet. Once, coming around a bend, he shied abruptly, like a startled horse, curved away from the place where he had been walking, and retreated several paces back along the trail. The creek he knew was frozen clear to the bottom—no creek could contain water in that arctic winter—but he knew also that there were springs that bubbled out from the hillsides and ran along under the snow and on top the ice of the creek. He knew that the coldest snaps never froze these springs, and he knew likewise their danger. They were traps. They hid pools of water under the snow that might be three inches deep, or three feet. Sometimes a skin of ice half an inch thick covered them, and in turn was covered by the snow. Sometimes there were alternate layers of water and ice-skin, so that when one broke through he kept on breaking through, for a while, sometimes wetting himself to the waist.

That was why he had shied in such panic. He had felt the give under his feet and heard the crackle of a snow-hidden ice-skin. And to get his feet wet in such a temperature meant trouble and danger. At the very least it meant delay, for he would be forced to stop and build a fire, and under its protection to bare his feet while he dried his socks and moccasins. He stood and studied the creek-bed and its banks, and decided that the flow of water came from the right. He reflected awhile, rubbing his nose and cheeks, then **skirted** to the left, stepping gingerly and testing the footing for each step. Once clear of the danger, he took a fresh chew of tobacco and swung along at his four-mile gait.

In the course of the next two hours, he came upon several similar traps. Usually the snow above the hidden pools had a sunken, candied appearance that advertised the danger. Once again, however, he had a close call; and once, suspecting danger, he compelled the dog to go on in front. The dog did not want to go. It hung back until the man shoved it forward, and then it went quickly across the white, unbroken surface. Suddenly it broke through, floundered to one side, and got away to firmer footing. It had wet its forefeet and legs, and almost immediately the water that clung to it turned to ice. It made quick efforts to lick the ice off its legs, then dropped down in the snow and began to bite out the ice that had formed between the toes. This was a matter of instinct. To permit the ice to remain would mean sore feet. It did not know this. It merely obeyed the mysterious prompting that arose from the deep crypts of its being. But the man knew, having achieved a judgment on the subject, and he removed the mitten from his right hand and helped tear out the ice- particles. He did not expose his fingers more than a minute, and was astonished at the swift numbness that **smote** them. It certainly was cold. He pulled on the mitten hastily and beat the hand savagely across his chest.

At twelve o'clock, the day was at its brightest. Yet the sun was too far south on its winter journey to clear the horizon. The bulge of the earth intervened between it and Henderson Creek, where the man walked under a clear sky at noon and cast no shadow. At half-past twelve, to the minute, he arrived at the forks of the creek. He was pleased at

Skirted: evaded, moved by

Smote: past tense of "smite," which means to hit hard

the speed he had made. If he kept it up, he would certainly be with the boys by six. He unbuttoned his jacket and shirt and drew forth his lunch. The action consumed no more than a quarter of a minute, yet in that brief moment the numbness laid hold of the exposed fingers. He did not put the mitten on, but, instead, struck the fingers a dozen sharp smashes against his leg. Then he sat down on a snow-covered log to eat. The sting that followed upon the striking of his fingers against his leg ceased so quickly that he was startled; he had had no chance to take a bite of biscuit. He struck the fingers repeatedly and returned them to the mitten, baring the other hand for the purpose of eating. He tried to take a mouthful, but the ice-muzzle prevented. He had forgotten to build a fire and thaw out. He chuckled at his foolishness, and as he chuckled he noted the numbness creeping into the exposed fingers. Also, he noted that the stinging which had first come to his toes when he sat down was already passing away. He wondered whether the toes were warm or numb. He moved them inside the moccasins and decided that they were numbed.

15   He pulled the mitten on hurriedly and stood up. He was a bit frightened. He stamped up and down until the stinging returned into the feet. It certainly was cold, was his thought. That man from Sulphur Creek had spoken the truth when telling how cold it sometimes got in the country. And he had laughed at him at the time! That showed one must not be too sure of things. There was no mistake about it, it was cold. He strode up and down, stamping his feet and threshing his arms, until reassured by the returning warmth. Then he got out matches and proceeded to make a fire. From the undergrowth, where high water of the previous spring had lodged a supply of seasoned twigs, he got his firewood. Working carefully from a small beginning, he soon had a roaring fire, over which he thawed the ice from his face and in the protection of which he ate his biscuits. For the moment the cold

of space was outwitted. The dog took satisfaction in the fire, stretching out close enough for warmth and far enough away to escape being singed.

When the man had finished, he filled his pipe and took his comfortable time over a smoke. Then he pulled on his mittens, settled the earflaps of his cap firmly about his ears, and took the creek trail up the left fork. The dog was disappointed and yearned back toward the fire. This man did not know cold. Possibly all the generations of his ancestry had been ignorant of cold, of real cold, of cold one hundred and seven degrees below freezing-point. But the dog knew; all its ancestry knew, and it had inherited the knowledge. And it knew that it was not good to walk abroad in such fearful cold. It was the time to lie snug in a hole in the snow and wait for a curtain of cloud to be drawn across the face of outer space from whence this cold came. On the other hand, there was keen intimacy between the dog and the man. The one was the toil-slave of the other, and the only caresses it had ever received were the caresses of the whiplash and of harsh and menacing throat-sounds that threatened the whiplash. So the dog made no effort to communicate its apprehension to the man. It was not concerned for the welfare of the man; it was for its own sake that it yearned back toward the fire. But the man whistled, and spoke to it with the sound of whiplashes, and the dog swung in at the man's heels and followed after.

The man took a chew of tobacco and proceeded to start a new amber beard. Also, his moist breath quickly powdered with white his moustache, eyebrows, and lashes. There did not seem to be so many springs on the left fork of the Henderson, and for half an hour the man saw no signs of any. And then it happened. At a place where there were no signs, where the soft, unbroken snow seemed to advertise solidity beneath, the man broke through. It was not deep. He wetted himself half-way to the knees before he floundered out to the firm crust.

He was angry, and cursed his luck aloud. He had hoped to get into camp with the boys at six

Imperative: essential, crucial

o'clock, and this would delay him an hour, for he would have to build a fire and dry out his foot gear. This was **imperative** at that low temperature—he knew that much; and he turned aside to the bank, which he climbed. On top, tangled in the underbrush about the trunks of several small spruce trees, was a high-water deposit of dry firewood—sticks and twigs principally, but also larger portions of seasoned branches and fine, dry, last-year's grasses. He threw down several large pieces on top of the snow. This served for a foundation and prevented the young flame from drowning itself in the snow it otherwise would melt. The flame he got by touching a match to a small shred of birch-bark that he took from his pocket. This burned even more readily than paper. Placing it on the foundation, he fed the young flame with wisps of dry grass and with the tiniest dry twigs.

He worked slowly and carefully, keenly aware of his danger. Gradually, as the flame grew stronger, he increased the size of the twigs with which he fed it. He squatted in the snow, pulling the twigs out from their entanglement in the brush and feeding directly to the flame. He knew there must be no failure. When it is seventy-five below zero, a man must not fail in his first attempt to build a fire—that is, if his feet are wet. If his feet are dry, and he fails, he can run along the trail for half a mile and restore his circulation. But the circulation of wet and freezing feet cannot be restored by running when it is seventy-five below. No matter how fast he runs, the wet feet will freeze the harder.

20   All this the man knew. The old-timer on Sulphur Creek had told him about it the previous fall, and now he was appreciating the advice. Already all sensation had gone out of his feet. To build the fire he had been forced to remove his mittens, and the fingers had quickly gone numb. His pace of four miles an hour had kept his heart pumping blood to the surface of his body and to all the extremities. But the instant he stopped,

the action of the pump eased down. The cold of space smote the unprotected tip of the planet, and he, being on that unprotected tip, received the full force of the blow. The blood of his body recoiled before it. The blood was alive, like the dog, and like the dog it wanted to hide away and cover itself up from the fearful cold. So long as he walked four miles an hour, he pumped that blood, willy-nilly, to the surface; but now it **ebbed** away and sank down into the recesses of his body. The extremities were the first to feel its absence. His wet feet froze the faster, and his exposed fingers numbed the faster, though they had not yet begun to freeze. Nose and cheeks were already freezing, while the skin of all his body chilled as it lost its blood.

Ebbed: lessened, declined, withdrew

But he was safe. Toes and nose and cheeks would be only touched by the frost, for the fire was beginning to burn with strength. He was feeding it with twigs the size of his finger. In another minute he would be able to feed it with branches the size of his wrist, and then he could remove his wet foot-gear, and, while it dried, he could keep his naked feet warm by the fire, rubbing them at first, of course, with snow. The fire was a success. He was safe. He remembered the advice of the old-timer on Sulphur Creek, and smiled. The old-timer had been very serious in laying down the law that no man must travel alone in the Klondike after fifty below. Well, here he was; he had had the accident; he was alone; and he had saved himself. Those old-timers were rather womanish, some of them, he thought. All a man had to do was to keep his head, and he was all right. Any man who was a man could travel alone. But it was surprising, the rapidity with which his cheeks and nose were freezing. And he had not thought his fingers could go lifeless in so short a time. Lifeless they were, for he could scarcely make them move together to grip a twig, and they seemed remote from his body and from him. When he touched a twig, he had to look and see whether or not he had hold of it. The wires were pretty well down between him and his finger-ends.

Conflagration: a massive fire

Imperceptible: unnoticed; unable to be measured

All of which counted for little. There was the fire, snapping and crackling and promising life with every dancing flame. He started to untie his moccasins. They were coated with ice; the thick German socks were like sheaths of iron half-way to the knees; and the moccasin strings were like rods of steel all twisted and knotted as by some **conflagration**. For a moment he tugged with his numbed fingers, then, realizing the folly of it, he drew his sheath-knife.

But before he could cut the strings, it happened. It was his own fault or, rather, his mistake. He should not have built the fire under the spruce tree. He should have built it in the open. But it had been easier to pull the twigs from the brush and drop them directly on the fire. Now the tree under which he had done this carried a weight of snow on its boughs. No wind had blown for weeks, and each bough was fully freighted. Each time he had pulled a twig he had communicated a slight agitation to the tree—an **imperceptible** agitation, so far as he was concerned, but an agitation sufficient to bring about the disaster. High up in the tree one bough capsized its load of snow. This fell on the boughs beneath, capsizing them. This process continued, spreading out and involving the whole tree. It grew like an avalanche, and it descended without warning upon the man and the fire, and the fire was blotted out! Where it had burned was a mantle of fresh and disordered snow.

The man was shocked. It was as though he had just heard his own sentence of death. For a moment he sat and stared at the spot where the fire had been. Then he grew very calm. Perhaps the old-timer on Sulphur Creek was right. If he had only had a trail-mate he would have been in no danger now. The trailmate could have built the fire. Well, it was up to him to build the fire over again, and this second time there must be no failure. Even if he succeeded, he would most likely lose some toes. His feet must be badly frozen by now, and there would be some time before the second fire was ready.

25   Such were his thoughts, but he did not sit and think them. He was busy all the time they were passing through his mind, he made a new foundation for a fire, this time in the open; where no treacherous tree could blot it out. Next, he gathered dry grasses and tiny twigs from the high-water **flotsam**. He could not bring his fingers together to pull them out, but he was able to gather them by the handful. In this way he got many rotten twigs and bits of green moss that were undesirable, but it was the best he could do. He worked methodically, even collecting an armful of the larger branches to be used later when the fire gathered strength. And all the while the dog sat and watched him, a certain yearning wistfulness in its eyes, for it looked upon him as the fire-provider, and the fire was slow in coming.

Flotsam: debris on water

When all was ready, the man reached in his pocket for a second piece of birch-bark. He knew the bark was there, and, though he could not feel it with his fingers, he could hear its crisp rustling as he fumbled for it. Try as he would, he could not clutch hold of it. And all the time, in his consciousness, was the knowledge that each instant his feet were freezing. This thought tended to put him in a panic, but he fought against it and kept calm. He pulled on his mittens with his teeth, and threshed his arms back and forth, beating his hands with all his might against his sides. He did this sitting down, and he stood up to do it; and all the while the dog sat in the snow, its wolf-brush of a tail curled around warmly over its forefeet, its sharp wolf-ears pricked forward intently as it watched the man. And the man as he beat and threshed with his arms and hands, felt a great surge of envy as he regarded the creature that was warm and secure in its natural covering.

After a time he was aware of the first far-away signals of sensation in his beaten fingers. The faint tingling grew stronger till it evolved into a stinging ache that was excruciating, but which the man hailed with satisfaction. He stripped the mitten from his right hand and fetched forth the birch bark. The exposed fingers were quickly going numb again. Next he brought out his bunch of sulphur matches. But the tremendous cold had already driven the life out of his fingers. In his effort to separate one match from the others, the whole bunch fell in the snow. He tried to pick it out of the snow, but failed. The dead fingers could neither touch nor clutch. He was very careful. He drove the thought of his freezing feet, and nose, and cheeks, out of his mind, devoting his whole soul to the matches. He watched, using the sense of vision in place of that of touch, and when he saw his fingers on each side the bunch, he closed them—that is, he willed to close them, for the wires were drawn, and the fingers did not obey. He pulled the mitten on the right hand, and beat it fiercely against his knee. Then, with both mittened hands, he scooped the bunch of matches, along with much snow, into his lap. Yet he was no better off.

After some manipulation, he managed to get the bunch between the heels of his mittened hands. In this fashion he carried it to his mouth. The ice crackled and snapped when by a violent effort he opened his mouth. He drew the lower jaw in, curled the upper lip out of the way, and scraped the bunch with his upper teeth in order to separate a match. He succeeded in getting one, which he dropped on his lap. He was no better off. He could not pick it up. Then he devised a way. He picked it up in his teeth and scratched it on his leg. Twenty times he scratched before he succeeded in lighting it. As it flamed, he held it with his teeth to the birch bark. But the burning **brimstone** went up his nostrils and into his lungs, causing him to cough **spasmodically**. The match fell into the snow and went out.

The old-timer on Sulphur Creek was right, he thought, in the moment of controlled despair that **ensued**: after fifty below, a man should travel with a partner. He beat his hands, but failed in exciting any sensation. Suddenly he bared both hands, removing the mittens with his teeth. He caught the

Brimstone: sulfur, which was used in matches

Spasmodically: violently; uncontrollably

Ensued: followed

whole bunch between the heels of his hands. His arm-muscles not being frozen enabled him to press the hand-heels tightly against the matches. Then he scratched the bunch along his leg. It flared into flame, seventy sulphur matches at once! There was no wind to blow them out. He kept his head to one side to escape the strangling fumes, and held the blazing bunch to the birch-bark. As he so held it, he became aware of sensation in his hand. His flesh was burning. He could smell it. Deep down below the surface he could feel it. The sensation developed into pain that grew **acute**. And still he endured it, holding the flame of the matches clumsily to the bark that would not light readily because his own burning hands were in the way, absorbing most of the flame.

Acute: sharp

30   At last, when he could endure no more, he jerked his hands apart. The blazing matches fell sizzling into the snow, but the birch-bark was alight. He began laying dry grasses and the tiniest twigs on the flame. He could not pick and choose, for he had to lift the fuel between the heels of his hands. Small pieces of rotten wood and green moss clung to the twigs, and he bit them off as well as he could with his teeth. He cherished the flame carefully and awkwardly. It meant life, and it must not perish. The withdrawal of blood from the surface of his body now made him begin to shiver, and he grew more awkward. A large piece of green moss fell squarely on the little fire. He tried to poke it out with his fingers, but his shivering frame made him poke too far, and he disrupted the nucleus of the little fire, the burning grasses and tiny twigs separating and scattering. He tried to poke them together again, but in spite of the tenseness of the effort, his shivering got away with him, and the twigs were hopelessly scattered. Each twig gushed a puff of smoke and went out. The fire-provider had failed. As he looked **apathetically** about him, his eyes chanced on the dog, sitting across the ruins of the fire from him, in the snow, making restless, hunching movements, slightly lifting one forefoot

Apathetically: indifferently

and then the other, shifting its weight back and forth on them with wistful eagerness.

The sight of the dog put a wild idea into his head. He remembered the tale of the man, caught in a blizzard, who killed a steer and crawled inside the carcass, and so was saved. He would kill the dog and bury his hands in the warm body until the numbness went out of them. Then he could build another fire. He spoke to the dog, calling it to him; but in his voice was a strange note of fear that frightened the animal, who had never known the man to speak in such way before. Something was the matter, and its suspicious nature sensed danger; it knew not what danger but somewhere, somehow, in its brain arose an apprehension of the man. It flattened its ears down at the sound of the man's voice, and its restless, hunching movements and the liftings and shiftings of its forefeet became more pronounced but it would not come to the man. He got on his hands and knees and crawled toward the dog. This unusual posture again excited suspicion, and the animal **sidled mincingly** away.

The man sat up in the snow for a moment and struggled for calmness. Then he pulled on his mittens, by means of his teeth, and got upon his feet. He glanced down at first in order to assure himself that he was really standing up, for the absence of sensation in his feet left him unrelated to the earth. His erect position in itself started to drive the webs of suspicion from the dog's mind; and when he spoke **peremptorily**, with the sound of whiplashes in his voice, the dog rendered its customary allegiance and came to him. As it came within reaching distance, the man lost his control. His arms flashed out to the dog, and he experienced genuine surprise when he discovered that his hands could not clutch, that there was neither bend nor feeling in the fingers. He had forgotten for the moment that they were frozen and that they were freezing more and more. All this happened quickly, and before the animal could get away, he encircled its body with his arms. He sat down in the snow,

Sidled: moved slowly sideways

Mincingly: in a very cautious manner, similar to tiptoeing

Peremptorily: in a way that prevents or restricts

and in this fashion held the dog, while it snarled and whined and struggled.

But it was all he could do, hold its body encircled in his arms and sit there. He realized that he could not kill the dog. There was no way to do it. With his helpless hands he could neither draw nor hold his sheath-knife nor **throttle** the animal. He released it, and it plunged wildly away, with tail between its legs, and still snarling. It halted forty feet away and surveyed him curiously, with ears sharply pricked forward. The man looked down at his hands in order to locate them, and found them hanging on the ends of his arms.

Throttle: to strangle

35   It struck him as curious that one should have to use his eyes in order to find out where his hands were. He began threshing his arms back and forth, beating the mittened hands against his sides. He did this for five minutes, violently, and his heart pumped enough blood up to the surface to put a stop to his shivering. But no sensation was aroused in the hands. He had an impression that they hung like weights on the ends of his arms, but when he tried to run the impression down, he could not find it.

A certain fear of death, dull and oppressive, came to him. This fear quickly became **poignant** as he realized that it was no longer a mere matter of freezing his fingers and toes, or of losing his hands and feet, but that it was a matter of life and death with the chances against him. This threw him into a panic, and he turned and ran up the creek bed along the old, dim trail. The dog joined in behind and kept up with him. He ran blindly, without intention, in fear such as he had never known in his life. Slowly, as he ploughed and floundered through the snow, he began to see things again—the banks of the creek, the old timberjams, the leafless aspens, and the sky. The running made him feel better. He did not shiver. Maybe, if he ran on, his feet would thaw out; and, anyway, if he ran far enough, he would reach camp and the boys. Without doubt he would lose some fingers and toes and some of his face; but the boys

Poignant: distressing; deep and powerful

would take care of him, and save the rest of him when he got there. And at the same time there was another thought in his mind that said he would never get to the camp and the boys; that it was too many miles away, that the freezing had too great a start on him, and that he would soon be stiff and dead. This thought he kept in the background and refused to consider. Sometimes it pushed itself forward and demanded to be heard, but he thrust it back and strove to think of other things.

It struck him as curious that he could run at all on feet so frozen that he could not feel them when they struck the earth and took the weight of his body. He seemed to himself to skim along above the surface and to have no connection with the earth. Somewhere he had once seen a winged Mercury, and he wondered if Mercury felt as he felt when skimming over the earth.

Mercury was the Roman god of commerce and the messenger of the gods.

His theory of running until he reached camp and the boys had one flaw in it: he lacked the endurance. Several times he stumbled, and finally he tottered, crumpled up, and fell. When he tried to rise, he failed. He must sit and rest, he decided, and next time he would merely walk and keep on going. As he sat and regained his breath, he noted that he was feeling quite warm and comfortable. He was not shivering, and it even seemed that a warm glow had come to his chest and trunk. And yet, when he touched his nose or cheeks, there was no sensation. Running would not thaw them out. Nor would it thaw out his hands and feet. Then the thought came to him that the frozen portions of his body must be extending. He tried to keep this thought down, to forget it, to think of something else; he was aware of the panicky feeling that it caused, and he was afraid of the panic. But the thought asserted itself, and persisted, until it produced a vision of his body totally frozen. This was too much, and he made another wild run along the trail. Once he slowed down to a walk, but the thought of the freezing extending itself made him run again.

And all the time the dog ran with him, at his heels. When he fell down a second time, it curled its tail over its forefeet and sat in front of him facing him curiously eager and intent. The warmth and security of the animal angered him, and he cursed it till it flattened down its ears **appeasingly**. This time the shivering came more quickly upon the man. He was losing in his battle with the frost. It was creeping into his body from all sides. The thought of it drove him on, but he ran no more than a hundred feet, when he staggered and pitched headlong. It was his last panic. When he had recovered his breath and control, he sat up and entertained in his mind the conception of meeting death with dignity. However, the conception did not come to him in such terms. His idea of it was that he had been making a fool of himself, running around like a chicken with its head cut off—such was the simile that occurred to him. Well, he was bound to freeze anyway, and he might as well take it decently. With this new-found peace of mind came the first glimmerings of drowsiness. A good idea, he thought, to sleep off to death. It was like taking an anaesthetic. Freezing was not so bad as people thought. There were lots worse ways to die.

He pictured the boys finding his body next day. Suddenly he found himself with them, coming along the trail and looking for himself. And, still with them, he came around a turn in the trail and found himself lying in the snow. He did not belong with himself any more, for even then he was out of himself, standing with the boys and looking at himself in the snow. It certainly was cold, was his thought. When he got back to the States he could tell the folks what real cold was. He drifted on from this to a vision of the old-timer on Sulphur Creek. He could see him quite clearly, warm and comfortable, and smoking a pipe.

"You were right, old hoss; you were right," the man mumbled to the old-timer of Sulphur Creek.

40   Then the man drowsed off into what seemed to him the most comfortable and satisfying sleep

Appeasingly: in a peaceful, placating manner

Chidden: scolded, reprimanded

Bristle: to get upset or aggravated

he had ever known. The dog sat facing him and waiting. The brief day drew to a close in a long, slow twilight. There were no signs of a fire to be made, and, besides, never in the dog's experience had it known a man to sit like that in the snow and make no fire. As the twilight drew on, its eager yearning for the fire mastered it, and with a great lifting and shifting of forefeet, it whined softly, then flattened its ears down in anticipation of being **chidden** by the man. But the man remained silent. Later, the dog whined loudly. And still later it crept close to the man and caught the scent of death. This made the animal **bristle** and back away. A little longer it delayed, howling under the stars that leaped and danced and shone brightly in the cold sky. Then it turned and trotted up the trail in the direction of the camp it knew, where were the other food-providers and fire-providers.

QUESTIONS

1. Have students watch the film version (1969, narrated by Orson Welles); they can then compare and contrast the original text with the movie in three objective, detailed paragraphs.

2. Analyze the impact of the author's choice of an objective, detached style of narration to develop and relate the elements of "To Build a Fire." How does this method affect the tone and overall impression?

3. The following quotation from paragraph 3 significantly adds to the characterization of the protagonist: "He was a newcomer in the land, a *Chechaquo*, and this was his first winter. The trouble with him was that he was without imagination." What can you infer from these statements regarding the man's environment and situation?

4. What are the effects of the author's choice to keep the main character anonymous?

5. Cite three instances where the ideas of "man versus nature" and "youth versus age" interact and build on one another to add to the complexity and power of the story.

6. Analyze how the connotations of the following word choices affect your opinion of the protagonist and his relationship with his dog: "suspecting danger, he compelled the dog to go on in front" (paragraph 13); "there was keen intimacy between the dog and the man. The one was the toil-slave of the other, and the only caresses it had ever received were the caresses of the whiplash and of harsh and menacing throat-sounds that threatened the whiplash" (paragraph 16).

Mark Twain

Luck

INTRODUCTION

Luck

This satirical tale of a very lucky, famous, and egotistical soldier is most likely based on a true story. Twain himself said that he had heard the story secondhand, and the common belief is that Twain's close friend Reverend Joseph Twichell told him about a bogus general whose supposed brilliant career was mostly the result of good fortune rather than intelligence. Twain wrote "Luck" in 1886 and published it in *Harper's* in 1891. The story was collected in *Merry Tales* the following year.

Mark Twain

Mark Twain had an ingenious knack for storytelling and self-promotion, and he made his living in his later years on the lecture circuit. Of course, Twain's hugely successful career and his amazing literary legacy are based on his many enduring publications and his deceivingly folksy ability to create both comedy and pathos almost simultaneously, as seen in his two most famous novels, *Tom Sawyer* (1876) and *Huckleberry Finn* (1884), the latter often called the "Great American Novel."

Samuel Langhorne Clemens took his pen name, Mark Twain, from a nautical measurement meaning two fathoms (12 feet)—shown as the second mark on a weighted line dropped into the water—which was a safe depth for a Mississippi riverboat to travel in. Born on November 30, 1835, in Florida, Missouri, about 40 miles from Hannibal, a port on the Mississippi, Clemens worked as an apprentice pilot and then a fully licensed pilot on riverboats from 1857 to 1861, when the Civil War brought a halt to regular traffic on the river.

A decade before he started his job on the Mississippi, Clemens had begun working as an assistant in his brother Orion's printing business in Hannibal. There, the young Clemens set type for a newspaper, and later, when Orion established his own newspaper in Iowa, Clemens worked for him there as well. In 1861, the brothers moved to Nevada; Clemens became a staff writer for the *Territorial Enterprise*, a newspaper in the mining town of Virginia City and started using his chosen pen name.

After relocating to San Francisco in 1864, Twain wrote for several newspapers, including *The Californian*. When one of his stories, "Jim Smiley and His Jumping Frog"—reprinted later that year as "The Celebrated Jumping Frog of Calaveras County"—was published by *The Saturday Press* in New York in 1865, it kick-started his career and was picked up by papers all across the country. During the next few years, Twain not only solidified his success as a writer, but he also became a popular speaker in New York City and the surrounding area. In 1867, Twain toured Europe and wrote a humorous, satirical account of his journey, which was published as *The Innocents Abroad* (1869) and became a bestseller.

Twain married Olivia (Livy) Langdon in 1870, and they would have four children, only one of whom lived a long life. The family settled in Hartford, Connecticut, where Twain produced his masterpieces about Tom and Huck, along with many other books and stories. While outwardly joyful and captivatingly witty, Twain had a dark side and was depressed for several years before his death. His downward emotional slide began when his favorite daughter, Susy, died; eight years later, he lost his wife to an illness, and in 1909, another daughter died. His son had passed away earlier.

Twain's deep cynicism is shown in such works as "The Man That Corrupted Hadleyburg" (1899) and *Letters from the Earth*, completed in 1909, but not published until 1962. His only surviving daughter, Clara, had refused to allow its publication, probably due to much of it being harshly anti-religious, but she finally relented, saying, "Mark Twain belonged to the world." On April 21, 1910, at the age of 74, Twain died of a heart attack.

Luck
Mark Twain (1866)

(NOTE—This is not a fancy sketch. I got it from a clergyman who was an instructor at Woolwich forty years ago, and who vouched for its truth.—M. T.)

IT WAS AT A BANQUET in London in honor of one of the two or three conspicuously illustrious English military names of this generation. For reasons which will presently appear, I will withhold his real name and titles and call him Lieutenant-General Lord Arthur Scoresby, V.C., K.C.B., etc., etc., etc. What a fascination there is in a renowned name! There sat the man, in actual flesh, whom I had heard of so many thousands of times since that day, thirty years before, when his name shot suddenly to the zenith from a Crimean battlefield, to remain forever celebrated. It was food and drink to me to look, and look, and look at that **demigod**; scanning, searching, noting: the quietness, the reserve, the noble gravity of his countenance; the simple honesty that expressed itself all over him; the sweet unconsciousness of his greatness—unconsciousness of the hundreds of admiring eyes fastened upon him, unconsciousness of the deep, loving, sincere worship welling out of the breasts of those people and flowing toward him.

The clergyman at my left was an old acquaintance of mine—clergyman now, but had spent the first half of his life in the camp and field and as an instructor in the military school at Woolwich. Just at the moment I have been talking about a veiled and singular light glimmered in his eyes and he leaned down and muttered confidentially to me—indicating the hero of the banquet with a gesture:

"Privately—he's an absolute fool."

This verdict was a great surprise to me. If its subject had been Napoleon, or Socrates, or Solomon, my astonishment could not have been greater. Two things I was well aware of: that the Reverend was

Demigod: a distinguished man who is idolized as if he were partly divine

Napoleon (1769-1821), an emperor of France, was a highly effective military commander; Socrates (469-399 BC), who taught Plato, helped form the basis for Western philosophy; Solomon (10th century BC), son of David, was a king of Israel well known for his wisdom.

a man of strict veracity and that his judgment of men was good. Therefore I knew, beyond doubt or question, that the world was mistaken about this hero: he was a fool. So I meant to find out, at a convenient moment, how the Reverend, all solitary and alone, had discovered the secret.

5 Some days later the opportunity came, and this is what the Reverend told me:

"About forty years ago I was an instructor in the military academy at Woolwich. I was present in one of the sections when young Scoresby underwent his preliminary examination. I was touched to the quick with pity, for the rest of the class answered up brightly and handsomely, while he—why, dear me, he didn't know *anything*, so to speak. He was evidently good, and sweet, and lovable, and guileless; and so it was exceedingly painful to see him stand there, as serene as a **graven image**, and deliver himself of answers which were **veritably** miraculous for stupidity and ignorance. All the compassion in me was aroused in his behalf. I said to myself, when he comes to be examined again he will be flung over, of course; so it will be simply a harmless act of charity to ease his fall as much as I can. I took him aside and found that he knew a little of Caesar's history, and as he didn't know anything else, I went to work and drilled him like a galley-slave on a certain line of stock questions concerning Caesar which I knew would be used. If you'll believe me, he went through with flying colors on examination day! He went through on that purely superficial "cram," and got compliments, too, while others, who knew a thousand times more than he, got plucked. By some strangely lucky accident—an accident not likely to happen twice in a century—he was asked no question outside of the narrow limits of his drill.

It was stupefying. Well, all through his course I stood by him, with something of the sentiment which a mother feels for a crippled child; and he always saved himself, just by miracle, apparently.

Graven image: an object of worship that is carved in stone or wood

Veritably: genuinely

Julius Caesar (100-44 BC), dictator of Rome, wrote a famous history of his conquests as a military leader.

Consternation: a feeling of shock and confusion

Preposterous: absolutely ridiculous

Prodigious: enormous, huge

Crimean War: The Crimean War (1853-1856) pitted Russia against Great Britain and its allies.

Sublimity: a high level of honor

Now, of course, the thing that would expose him and kill him at last was mathematics. I resolved to make his death as easy as I could; so I drilled him and crammed him, and crammed him and drilled him, just on the line of questions which the examiners would be most likely to use, and then launched him on his fate. Well, sir, try to conceive of the result: to my **consternation**, he took the first prize! And with it he got a perfect ovation in the way of compliments.

Sleep? There was no more sleep for me for a week. My conscience tortured me day and night. What I had done I had done purely through charity, and only to ease the poor youth's fall. I never had dreamed of any such **preposterous** results as the thing that had happened. I felt as guilty and miserable as Frankenstein. Here was a wooden-head whom I had put in the way of glittering promotions and **prodigious** responsibilities, and but one thing could happen: he and his responsibilities would all go to ruin together at the first opportunity

10   The **Crimean War** had just broken out. Of course there had to be a war, I said to myself. We couldn't have peace and give this donkey a chance to die before he is found out. I waited for the earthquake. It came. And it made me reel when it did come. He was actually gazetted to a captaincy in a marching regiment! Better men grow old and gray in the service before they climb to a **sublimity** like that. And who could ever have foreseen that they would go and put such a load of responsibility on such green and inadequate shoulders? I could just barely have stood it if they had made him a cornet, but a captain—think of it! I thought my hair would turn white.

Consider what I did—I who so loved repose and inaction. I said to myself, I am responsible to the country for this, and I must go along with him and protect the country against him as far as I can. So I took my poor little capital that I had saved up through years of work and grinding economy, and went with a sigh and bought a place in his regiment, and away we went to the field.

And there—oh, dear, it was awful. Blunders? Why, he never did anything but blunder. But, you see, nobody was in the fellow's secret—everybody had him focused wrong, and necessarily misinterpreted his performance every time—consequently they took his idiotic blunders for inspirations of genius; they did, honestly! His mildest blunders were enough to make a man in his right mind cry; and they did make me cry—and rage and rave, too, privately. And the thing that kept me always in a sweat of apprehension was the fact that every fresh blunder he made always increased the luster of his reputation! I kept saying to myself, He'll get so high that when discovery does finally come, it will be like the sun falling out of the sky.

He went right along up, from grade to grade, over the dead bodies of his superiors, until at last, in the hottest moment of the battle of—down went our colonel, and my heart jumped into my mouth, for Scoresby was next in rank! Now for it, said I; we'll all land in Sheol in ten minutes, sure.

The battle was awfully hot; the allies were steadily giving way all over the field. Our regiment occupied a position that was vital; a blunder now must be destruction. At this crucial moment, what does this immortal fool do, but detach the regiment from its place and order a charge over a neighboring hill where there wasn't a suggestion of an enemy! "There you go!" I said to myself; "this is the end at last."

15 And away we did go, and were over the shoulder of the hill before the insane movement could be discovered and stopped. And what did we find? An entire and unsuspected Russian army in reserve! And what happened? We were eaten up? That is necessarily what would have happened in ninety-nine cases out of a hundred. But no; those Russians argued that no single regiment would come browsing around there at such a time. It must be the entire English army, and that the sly Russian game was detected and blocked; so they turned tail, and away they went, **pell-mell**, over the hill

Pell-mell: in a hasty, disorderly way

105

Marshal Canrobert (1809-1895)
was a well-known French
commander. France was one
of Britain's allies during the
Crimean War.

and down into the field, in wild confusion, and we after them; they themselves broke the solid Russian center in the field, and tore through, and in no time there was the most tremendous rout you ever saw, and the defeat of the allies was turned into a sweeping and splendid victory! Marshal Canrobert looked on, dizzy with astonishment, admiration, and delight; and sent right off for Scoresby, and hugged him, and decorated him on the field in presence of all the armies!

And what was Scoresby's blunder that time? Merely the mistaking his right hand for his left—that was all. An order had come to him to fall back and support our right; and instead, he fell *forward* and went over the hill to the left. But the name he won that day as a marvelous military genius filled the world with his glory, and that glory will never fade while history books last.

He is just as good and sweet and lovable and unpretending as a man can be, but he doesn't know enough to come in when it rains. Now that is absolutely true. He is the supremest ass in the universe; and until half an hour ago nobody knew it but himself and me. He has been pursued, day by day and year by year, by a most phenomenal and astonishing luckiness. He has been a shining soldier in all our wars for a generation; he has littered his whole military life with blunders, and yet has never committed one that didn't make him a knight or a baronet or a lord or something. Look at his breast; why, he is just clothed in domestic and foreign decorations. Well, sir, every one of them is the record of some shouting stupidity or other; and, taken together, they are proof that the very best thing in all this world that can befall a man is to be born lucky. I say again, as I said at the banquet, Scoresby's an absolute fool.

QUESTIONS

1. Analyze how Mark Twain's changing of the point of view shortly after the beginning of the story (in paragraph 6) helps the reader understand that it is a satire. Who or what is the implied target of the satire?

2. How does Twain order the events to build momentum and increase the impact of the story's climax?

3. Describe the new meaning, connotations, and tone of the opening description of Scoresby after you have read "Luck." For example, why might the "real" general be showing "quietness" and "unconsciousness"?

4. What is the impact of Twain's choice of words when the first narrator calls the general a "demigod" and, soon afterward, the clergyman remembers him being "as serene as a graven image"?

5. Determine the two main themes of the story and, in a detailed, well-organized paragraph, write an objective summary focusing on how these themes increase the story's complexity and overall impact.

F. Scott Fitzgerald

The Ice Palace

INTRODUCTION

The Ice Palace

"The Ice Palace" was written in 1919 and, like many of Fitzgerald's works, was published in *The Saturday Evening Post* (May 22, 1920). He soon chose it as one of the eight stories for his first collection, *Flappers and Philosophers* (1920). The main character, Sally Carrol, is thought to have been modeled after Fitzgerald's wife, Zelda, who was from Montgomery, Alabama.

F. Scott Fitzgerald

In one of his notebooks, collected in *The Crack-Up* (1945), Fitzgerald said, "Vitality shows in not only the ability to persist but the ability to start over." He himself started over several times after alcoholism and excessive spending had derailed his career. He died of a heart attack at the age of 44. Nonetheless, in his 20 years of writing professionally, Fitzgerald had a great deal of success, especially with his continually popular short stories; he made a good living as a Hollywood screenwriter; and he wrote *The Great Gatsby* (1925), which has long been considered one of the top two greatest American novels (along with *Huckleberry Finn*). He had a stormy marriage to Zelda Sayre Fitzgerald, who suffered from mental illness, probably accelerated by alcohol use, and died in 1948. Fitzgerald is now recognized as one of the greatest American writers of fiction.

Born on September 24, 1896, in St. Paul, Minnesota, Francis Scott Key Fitzgerald was a distant relative of the famous writer of the National Anthem. Although Fitzgerald's father was a failure in business, the family lived well on his mother's inheritance from her father, a successful, large-scale grocer. Fitzgerald attended Princeton University, but preferring to write creatively instead of studying. In 1917, he was placed on academic probation and decided to join the army. He was never called to active duty but spent a few years crafting his first novel, *This Side of Paradise*, which was published in 1920 and quickly led to him becoming a wealthy and popular writer.

The "Roaring Twenties," which Fitzgerald called "The Jazz Age," offered him and his wife, Zelda, an opportunity to become world-famous party people who traveled between New York and Paris, quickly spending the thousands of dollars his writing regularly brought in. Fitzgerald met and developed a friendship with Ernest Hemingway, whom he introduced to his publishers, jump-starting Hemingway's career. After *The Great Gatsby*, though, Fitzgerald's own career took several nosedives, and he never returned to that great peak of success. In a July 1949 letter to Arthur Mizener, one of Fitzgerald's biographers, Hemingway noted that Fitzgerald "had a very steep trajectory and was almost like a guided missile with no one guiding him."

The Ice Palace
F. Scott Fitzgerald (1920)

I

THE SUNLIGHT DRIPPED over the house like golden paint over an art jar, and the freckling shadows here and there only intensified the rigor of the bath of light. The Butterworth and Larkin houses flanking were entrenched behind great **stodgy** trees; only the Happer house took the full sun, and all day long faced the dusty road-street with a tolerant kindly patience. This was the city of Tarleton in southernmost Georgia, September afternoon.

Stodgy: stubbornly old-fashioned

Up in her bedroom window Sally Carrol Happer rested her nineteen-year-old chin on a fifty-two-year-old sill and watched Clark Darrow's ancient Ford turn the corner. The car was hot—being partly metallic it retained all the heat it absorbed or evolved —and Clark Darrow sitting bolt upright at the wheel wore a pained, strained expression as though he considered himself a spare part, and rather likely to break. He laboriously crossed two dust ruts, the wheels squeaking indignantly at the encounter, and then with a terrifying expression he gave the steering-gear a final wrench and deposited self and car approximately in front of the Happer steps. There was a plaintive heaving sound, a death-rattle, followed by a short silence; and then the air was rent by a startling whistle.

Sally Carrol gazed down sleepily. She started to yawn, but finding this quite impossible unless she raised her chin from the window-sill, changed her mind and continued silently to regard the car, whose owner sat brilliantly if perfunctorily at attention as he waited for an answer to his signal. After a moment the whistle once more split the dusty air.

"Good mawnin'."

5   With difficulty Clark twisted his tall body round and bent a distorted glance on the window.

" 'Tain't mawnin', Sally Carrol."

"Isn't it, sure enough?"

"What you do in'?"

"Eatin' 'n apple."

10   "Come on go swimmin'—want to?"

"Reckon so."

"How 'bout hurryin' up?"

"Sure enough."

Sally Carrol sighed voluminously and raised herself with profound inertia from the floor, where she had been occupied in alternately destroying parts of a green apple and painting paper tops for her younger sister. She approached a mirror, regarded her expression with a pleased and pleasant languor, dabbed two spots of rouge on her lips and a grain of powder on her nose, and covered her bobbed corn-colored hair with a rose littered sun bonnet. Then she kicked over the painting water, said, "Oh, damn!" —but let it lay—and left the room.

15   "How you, Clark?" she inquired a minute later as she slipped nimbly over the side of the car.

"Mighty fine, Sally Carrol."

"Where we go swimmin'?"

"Out to Walley's pool. Told Marylyn we'd call by an' get her an' Joe Ewing."

Clark was dark and lean, and when on foot was rather inclined to stoop. His eyes were ominous and his expression somewhat **petulant** except when startlingly illuminated by one of his frequent smiles. Clark had "a income"—just enough to keep himself in ease and his car in gasolene—and he had spent the two years since he graduated from Georgia Tech in dozing round the lazy streets of his home town, discussing how he could best invest his capital for an immediate fortune.

20   Hanging round he found not at all difficult; a crowd of little girls had grown up beautifully, the amazing Sally Carrol foremost among them; and they enjoyed being swum with and danced with and made love to in the flower-filled summery evenings —and they all liked Clark immensely. When feminine company **palled** there were half a dozen other youths who were always just about to do something, and meanwhile were quite willing to join him in a few holes of golf, or a game of billiards,

Petulant: irritable

Palled: thinned out

or the consumption of a quart of "hard yella licker." Every once in a while one of these contemporaries made a farewell round of calls before going up to New York or Philadelphia or Pittsburgh to go into business, but mostly they just stayed round in this languid parade of dreamy skies and firefly evenings and noisy niggery street fairs—and especially of gracious, soft-voiced girls, who were brought up on memories instead of money.

The Ford having been excited into a sort of restless resentful life Clark and Sally Carrol rolled and rattled down Valley Avenue into Jefferson Street, where the dust road became a pavement; along **opiate** Millicent Place, where there were half a dozen prosperous, substantial mansions; and on into the down-town section. Driving was perilous here, for it was shopping time; the population idled casually across the streets and a drove of low-moaning oxen were being urged along in front of a placid street-car; even the shops seemed only yawning their doors and blinking their windows in the sunshine before retiring into a state of utter and finite coma.

Opiate: having the calming, numbing effect of a narcotic drug

"Sally Carrol," said Clark suddenly, "it a fact that you're engaged?"

She looked at him quickly.

"Where'd you hear that?"

25 "Sure enough, you engaged?"

" 'At's a nice question!"

"Girl told me you were engaged to a Yankee you met up in Asheville last summer."

Sally Carrol sighed.

"Never saw such an old town for rumors."

30 "Don't marry a Yankee, Sally Carrol. We need you round here."

Sally Carrol was silent a moment.

"Clark," she demanded suddenly, "who on earth shall I marry?"

"I offer my services."

"Honey, you couldn't support a wife," she answered cheerfully. "Anyway, I know you too well to fall in love with you."

Dilapidated: damaged by time and use; in disrepair

35   "'At doesn't mean you ought to marry a Yankee," he persisted.

"S'pose I love him?"

He shook his head.

"You couldn't. He'd be a lot different from us, every way."

He broke off as he halted the car in front of a rambling, **dilapidated** house. Marylyn Wade and Joe Ewing appeared in the doorway.

40   " 'Lo, Sally Carrol."

"Hi!"

"How you-all?"

"Sally Carrol," demanded Marylyn as they started off again, "you engaged?"

"Lawdy, where'd all this start? Can't I look at a man 'thout everybody in town engagin' me to him?"

45   Clark stared straight in front of him at a bolt on the clattering wind-shield.

"Sally Carrol," he said with a curious intensity, "don't you like us?"

"What?"

"Us down here?"

"Why, Clark, you know I do. I adore all you boys."

50   "Then why you gettin' engaged to a Yankee?"

"Clark, I don't know. I'm not sure what I'll do, but—well, I want to go places and see people. I want my mind to grow. I want to live where things happen on a big scale."

"What you mean?"

"Oh, Clark, I love you, and I love Joe here, and Ben Arrot, and you-all, but you'll—you'll—"

"We'll all be failures?"

55   "Yes. I don't mean only money failures, but just sort of—of ineffectual and sad, and—oh, how can I tell you?"

"You mean because we stay here in Tarleton?"

"Yes, Clark; and because you like it and never want to change things or think or go ahead."

He nodded and she reached over and pressed his hand.

"Clark," she said softly, "I wouldn't change you for the world. You're sweet the way you are.

The things that'll make you fail I'll love always—
the living in the past, the lazy days and nights you
have, and all your carelessness and generosity."

60   "But you're goin' away?"

"Yes—because I couldn't ever marry you.
You've a place in my heart no one else ever could
have, but tied down here I'd get restless. I'd feel I
was—wastin' myself. There's two sides to me, you
see. There's the sleepy old side you love; an' there's
a sort of energy—the feelin' that makes me do wild
things. That's the part of me that may be useful
somewhere, that'll last when I'm not beautiful any
more."

She broke off with characteristic suddenness
and sighed, "Oh, sweet cooky!" as her mood
changed.

Half closing her eyes and tipping back her
head till it rested on the seat-back she let the savory
breeze fan her eyes and ripple the fluffy curls of
her bobbed hair. They were in the country now,
hurrying between tangled growths of bright-green
coppice and grass and tall trees that sent sprays of
foliage to hang a cool welcome over the road. Here
and there they passed a battered negro cabin, its
oldest white-haired inhabitant smoking a corncob
pipe beside the door, and half a dozen scantily
clothed pickaninnies parading tattered dolls on
the wild-grown grass in front. Farther out were
lazy cotton-fields, where even the workers seemed
intangible shadows lent by the sun to the earth, not
for toil, but to while away some age-old tradition in
the golden September fields. And round the drowsy
picturesqueness, over the trees and shacks and
muddy rivers, flowed the heat, never hostile, only
comforting, like a great warm nourishing bosom for
the infant earth.

"Sally Carrol, we're here!" "Poor chile's soun'
asleep."

65   "Honey, you dead at last out a sheer laziness?"

"Water, Sally Carrol! Cool water waitin' for you!"

Her eyes opened sleepily.

"Hi!" she murmured, smiling.

II

IN NOVEMBER HARRY BELLAMY, tall, broad, and brisk, came down from his Northern city to spend four days. His intention was to settle a matter that had been hanging fire since he and Sally Carrol had met in Asheville, North Carolina, in midsummer. The settlement took only a quiet afternoon and an evening in front of a glowing open fire, for Harry Bellamy had everything she wanted; and, besides, she loved him—loved him with that side of her she kept especially for loving. Sally Carrol had several rather clearly defined sides.

On his last afternoon they walked, and she found their steps tending half-unconsciously toward one of her favorite haunts, the cemetery. When it came in sight, gray-white and golden-green under the cheerful late sun, she paused, irresolute, by the iron gate.

"Are you mournful by nature, Harry?" she asked with a faint smile.

"Mournful? Not I."

5   "Then let's go in here. It depresses some folks, but I like it."

They passed through the gateway and followed a path that led through a wavy valley of graves—dusty-gray and mouldy for the fifties; quaintly carved with flowers and jars for the seventies; ornate and hideous for the nineties, with fat marble cherubs lying in sodden sleep on stone pillows, and great impossible growths of nameless granite flowers.

Occasionally they saw a kneeling figure with tributary flowers, but over most of the graves lay silence and withered leaves with only the fragrance that their own shadowy memories could waken in living minds.

They reached the top of a hill where they were fronted by a tall, round head-stone, freckled with dark spots of damp and half grown over with vines.

"Margery Lee," she read; "1844-1873. Wasn't she nice? She died when she was twenty-nine. Dear Margery Lee," she added softly. "Can't you see her, Harry?"

The gravestones are described in terms of when they were put in place. The "fifties" refers to the 1850s because "The Ice Palace" is set in 1920.

10 "Yes, Sally Carrol."

He felt a little hand insert itself into his.

"She was dark, I think; and she always wore her hair with a ribbon in it, and gorgeous hoop-skirts of Alice blue and old rose."

"Yes."

"Oh, she was sweet, Harry! And she was the sort of girl born to stand on a wide, pillared porch and welcome folks in. I think perhaps a lot of men went away to war meanin' to come back to her; but maybe none of 'em ever did."

15 He stooped down close to the stone, hunting for any record of marriage.

"There's nothing here to show."

"Of course not. How could there be anything there better than just 'Margery Lee,' and that eloquent date?"

She drew close to him and an unexpected lump came into his throat as her yellow hair brushed his cheek.

"You see how she was, don't you, Harry?"

20 "I see," he agreed gently. "I see through your precious eyes. You're beautiful now, so I know she must have been."

Silent and close they stood, and he could feel her shoulders trembling a little. An ambling breeze swept up the hill and stirred the brim of her floppidy hat.

"Let's go down there!"

She was pointing to a flat stretch on the other side of the hill where along the green-turf were a thousand grayish-white crosses stretching in endless, ordered rows like the stacked arms of a battalion.

"Those are the Confederate dead," said Sally Carrol simply.

25 They walked along and read the inscriptions, always only a name and a date, sometimes quite **indecipherable**.

"The last row is the saddest—see, 'way over there. Every cross has just a date on it, and the word 'Unknown.'"

Indecipherable: not able to be understood

She looked at him and her eyes brimmed with tears.

"I can't tell you how real it is to me, darling—if you don't know."

"How you feel about it is beautiful to me."

30   "No, no, it's not me, it's them—that old time that I've tried to have live in me. These were just men, unimportant evidently or they wouldn't have been 'unknown'; but they died for the most beautiful thing in the world—the dead South. You see," she continued, her voice still husky, her eyes glistening with tears, "people have these dreams they fasten onto things, and I've always grown up with that dream. It was so easy because it was all dead and there weren't any disillusions comin' to me. I've tried in a way to live up to those past standards of noblesse oblige—there's just the last remnants of it, you know, like the roses of an old garden dying all round us—streaks of strange courtliness and chivalry in some of these boys an' stories I used to hear from a Confederate soldier who lived next door, and a few old darkies. Oh, Harry, there was something, there was something! I couldn't ever make you understand, but it was there."

"I understand," he assured her again quietly.

Sally Carrol smiled and dried her eyes on the tip of a handkerchief protruding from his breast pocket.

"You don't feel depressed, do you, lover? Even when I cry I'm happy here, and I get a sort of strength from it."

Hand in hand they turned and walked slowly away. Finding soft grass she drew him down to a seat beside her with their backs against the remnants of a low broken wall.

35   "Wish those three old women would clear out," he complained. "I want to kiss you, Sally Carrol."

"Me, too."

They waited impatiently for the three bent figures to move off, and then she kissed him until the sky seemed to fade out and all her smiles and tears to vanish in an ecstasy of eternal seconds.

Afterward they walked slowly back together, while on the corners twilight played at somnolent black-and-white checkers with the end of day.

"You'll be up about mid-January," he said, "and you've got to stay a month at least. It'll be slick. There's a winter carnival on, and if you've never really seen snow it'll be like fairy-land to you. There'll be skating and skiing and tobogganing and sleigh-riding, and all sorts of torchlight parades on snow-shoes. They haven't had one for years, so they're going to make it a knock-out."

40   "Will I be cold, Harry?" she asked suddenly.

"You certainly won't. You may freeze your nose, but you won't be shivery cold. It's hard and dry, you know."

"I guess I'm a summer child. I don't like any cold I've ever seen."

She broke off and they were both silent for a minute.

"Sally Carrol," he said very slowly, "what do you say to—March?"

45   "I say I love you."

"March?"

"March, Harry."

III

ALL NIGHT IN THE **Pullman** it was very cold. She rang for the porter to ask for another blanket, and when he couldn't give her one she tried vainly, by squeezing down into the bottom of her berth and doubling back the bedclothes, to snatch a few hours' sleep. She wanted to look her best in the morning.

She rose at six and sliding uncomfortably into her clothes stumbled up to the diner for a cup of coffee. The snow had filtered into the **vestibules** and covered the floor with a slippery coating. It was intriguing, this cold, it crept in everywhere. Her breath was quite visible and she blew into the air with a naïve enjoyment. Seated in the diner she stared out the window at white hills and valleys and

Pullman: a train car with bunk beds

Vestibules: closed-in spaces between railway cars

scattered pines whose every branch was a green platter for a cold feast of snow. Sometimes a solitary farmhouse would fly by, ugly and bleak and lone on the white waste; and with each one she had an instant of chill compassion for the souls shut in there waiting for spring.

As she left the diner and swayed back into the Pullman she experienced a surging rush of energy and wondered if she was feeling the bracing air of which Harry had spoken. This was the North, the North—her land now!

"Then blow, ye winds, heigho! A-roving I will go," she chanted exultantly to herself.

"What's 'at?" inquired the porter politely.

5   "I said: 'Brush me off.'"

The long wires of the telegraph-poles doubled; two tracks ran up beside the train—three—four; came a succession of white-roofed houses, a glimpse of a trolley-car with frosted windows, streets—more streets—the city.

She stood for a dazed moment in the frosty station before she saw three fur-bundled figures descending upon her.

"There she is!"

"Oh, Sally Carrol!"

10   Sally Carrol dropped her bag.

"Hi!"

A faintly familiar icy-cold face kissed her, and then she was in a group of faces all apparently emitting great clouds of heavy smoke; she was shaking hands. There were Gordon, a short, eager man of thirty who looked like an amateur knocked-about model for Harry, and his wife, Myra, a listless lady with flaxen hair under a fur automobile cap. Almost immediately Sally Carrol thought of her as vaguely Scandinavian. A cheerful chauffeur adopted her bag, and amid ricochets of half-phrases, exclamations, and perfunctory listless "my dears" from Myra, they swept each other from the station.

Then they were in a sedan bound through a crooked succession of snowy streets where dozens of little boys were hitching sleds behind grocery wagons and automobiles.

15   "Oh," cried Sally Carrol, "I want to do that! Can we, Harry?"

"That's for kids. But we might—"

"It looks like such a circus" she said regretfully.

Home was a rambling frame house set on a white lap of snow, and there she met a big, gray-haired man of whom she approved, and a lady who was like an egg, and who kissed her—these were Harry's parents. There was a breathless indescribable hour crammed full of half-sentences, hot water, bacon and eggs and confusion; and after that she was alone with Harry in the library, asking him if she dared smoke.

It was a large room with a Madonna over the fireplace and rows upon rows of books in covers of light gold and dark gold and shiny red. All the chairs had little lace squares where one's head should rest, the couch was just comfortable, the books looked as if they had been read—some— and Sally Carrol had an instantaneous vision of the battered old library at home, with her father's huge medical books, and the oil-paintings of her three great-uncles, and the old couch that had been mended up for forty-five years and was still luxurious to dream in. This room struck her as being neither attractive nor particularly otherwise. It was simply a room with a lot of fairly expensive things in it that all looked about fifteen years old.

20   "What do you think of it up here?" demanded Harry eagerly. "Does it surprise you? Is it what you expected, I mean?"

"You are, Harry," she said quietly, and reached out her arms to him.

But after a brief kiss he seemed anxious to extort enthusiasm from her.

"The town, I mean. Do you like it? Can you feel the pep in the air?"

"Oh, Harry," she laughed, "you'll have to give me time. You can't just fling questions at me."

25   She puffed at her cigarette with a sigh of contentment.

"One thing I want to ask you," he began rather apologetically; "you Southerners put quite an emphasis on family, and all that—not that it isn't quite all right, but you'll find it a little different here. I mean—you'll notice a lot of things that'll seem to you sort of vulgar display at first, Sally Carrol; but just remember that this is a three-generation town. Everybody has a father, and about half of us have grandfathers. Back of that we don't go."

"Of course," she murmured.

"Our grandfathers, you see, founded the place, and a lot of them had to take some pretty queer jobs while they were doing the founding. For instance, there's one woman who at present is about the social model for the town; well, her father was the first public **ash man**—things like that."

Ash man: a collector of ashes and other garbage

"Why," said Sally Carrol, puzzled, "did you s'pose I was goin' to make remarks about people?"

30   "Not at all," interrupted Harry; "and I'm not apologizing for any one either. It's just that—well, a Southern girl came up here last summer and said some unfortunate things, and—oh, I just thought I'd tell you."

Sally Carrol felt suddenly indignant—as though she had been unjustly spanked—but Harry evidently considered the subject closed, for he went on with a great surge of enthusiasm.

"It's carnival time, you know. First in ten years. And there's an ice palace they're building now that's the first they've had since eighty-five. Built out of blocks of the clearest ice they could find—on a tremendous scale."

She rose and walking to the window pushed aside the heavy Turkish **portires** and looked out.

Portires: thick curtains

"Oh!" she cried suddenly. "There's two little boys makin' a snow man! Harry, do you reckon I can go out an' help 'em?"

35   "You dream! Come here and kiss me."

She left the window rather reluctantly.

"I don't guess this is a very kissable climate, is it? I mean, it makes you so you don't want to sit round, doesn't it?"

"We're not going to. I've got a vacation for the first week you're here, and there's a dinner-dance to-night."

"Oh, Harry," she confessed, subsiding in a heap, half in his lap, half in the pillows, "I sure do feel confused. I haven't got an idea whether I'll like it or not, an' I don't know what people expect, or anythin'. You'll have to tell me, honey."

40   "I'll tell you," he said softly, "if you'll just tell me you're glad to be here."

"Glad—just awful glad!" she whispered, **insinuating** herself into his arms in her own peculiar way. "Where you are is home for me, Harry."

Insinuating: moving in a gradual, subtle way

And as she said this she had the feeling for almost the first time in her life that she was acting a part.

That night, amid the gleaming candles of a dinner-party, where the men seemed to do most of the talking while the girls sat in a haughty and expensive aloofness, even Harry's presence on her left failed to make her feel at home.

"They're a good-looking crowd, don't you think?" he demanded. "Just look round. There's Spud Hubbard, tackle at Princeton last year, and Junie Morton—he and the red-haired fellow next to him were both Yale hockey captains; Junie was in my class. Why, the best athletes in the world come from these States round here. This is a man's country, I tell you. Look at John J. Fishburn!"

45   "Who's he?" asked Sally Carrol innocently.

"Don't you know?"

"I've heard the name."

"Greatest wheat man in the Northwest, and one of the greatest financiers in the country."

She turned suddenly to a voice on her right.

50   "I guess they forgot to introduce us. My name's Roger Patton."

"My name is Sally Carrol Happer," she said graciously.

"Yes, I know. Harry told me you were coming."

"You a relative?"

"No, I'm a professor."

55   "Oh," she laughed.

"At the university. You're from the South, aren't you?"

"Yes; Tarleton, Georgia."

She liked him immediately—a reddish-brown mustache under watery blue eyes that had something in them that these other eyes lacked, some quality of appreciation. They exchanged stray sentences through dinner, and she made up her mind to see him again.

After coffee she was introduced to numerous good-looking young men who danced with conscious precision and seemed to take it for granted that she wanted to talk about nothing except Harry.

60   "Heavens," she thought, "they talk as if my being engaged made me older than they are—as if I'd tell their mothers on them!"

In the South an engaged girl, even a young married woman, expected the same amount of half-affectionate **badinage** and flattery that would be accorded a debutante, but here all that seemed banned. One young man, after getting well started on the subject of Sally Carrol's eyes, and how they had allured him ever since she entered the room, went into a violent confusion when he found she was visiting the Bellamys—was Harry's fiancée. He seemed to feel as though he had made some **risqué** and inexcusable blunder, became immediately formal, and left her at the first opportunity.

She was rather glad when Roger Patton cut in on her and suggested that they sit out a while.

"Well," he inquired, blinking cheerily, "how's Carmen from the South?"

"Mighty fine. How's—how's Dangerous Dan McGrew? Sorry, but he's the only Northerner I know much about."

65   He seemed to enjoy that.

Badinage: light conversation

Risqué: somewhat vulgar

"Of course," he confessed, "as a professor of literature I'm not supposed to have read Dangerous Dan McGrew."

"Are you a native?"

"No, I'm a Philadelphian. Imported from Harvard to teach French. But I've been here ten years."

"Nine years, three hundred and sixty-four days longer than me."

70 "Like it here?"

"Uh-huh. Sure do!"

"Really?"

"Well, why not? Don't I look as if I were havin' a good time?"

"I saw you look out the window a minute ago—and shiver."

75 "Just my imagination," laughed Sally Carrol. "I'm used to havin' everythin' quiet outside, an' sometimes I look out an' see a flurry of snow, an' it's just as if somethin' dead was movin'."

He nodded appreciatively.

"Ever been North before?"

"Spent two Julys in Asheville, North Carolina."

"Nice-looking crowd, aren't they?" suggested Patton, indicating the swirling floor.

80 Sally Carrol started. This had been Harry's remark.

"Sure are! They're—canine."

"What?"

She flushed.

"I'm sorry; that sounded worse than I meant it. You see I always think of people as feline or canine, irrespective of sex."

85 "Which are you?"

"I'm feline. So are you. So are most Southern men an' most of these girls here."

"What's Harry?"

"Harry's canine distinctly. All the men I've met to-night seem to be canine."

"What does 'canine' imply? A certain conscious masculinity as opposed to subtlety?"

90 "Reckon so. I never analyzed it—only I just look at people an' say 'canine' or 'feline' right off. It's right absurd, I guess."

Ibsenesque: resembling
the characters created by
Norwegian playwright
Henrik Ibsen

"Not at all. I'm interested. I used to have a theory about these people. I think they're freezing up."

"What?"

"I think they're growing like Swedes—**Ibsenesque**, you know. Very gradually getting gloomy and melancholy. It's these long winters. Ever read any Ibsen?"

She shook her head.

95 "Well, you find in his characters a certain brooding rigidity. They're righteous, narrow, and cheerless, without infinite possibilities for great sorrow or joy."

"Without smiles or tears?"

"Exactly. That's my theory. You see there are thousands of Swedes up here. They come, I imagine, because the climate is very much like their own, and there's been a gradual mingling. There're probably not half a dozen here to-night, but—we've had four Swedish governors. Am I boring you?'

"I'm mighty interested."

"Your future sister-in-law is half Swedish. Personally I like her, but my theory is that Swedes react rather badly on us as a whole. Scandinavians, you know, have the largest suicide rate in the world."

75 "Why do you live here if it's so depressing?"

"Oh, it doesn't get me. I'm pretty well cloistered, and I suppose, books mean more than people to me anyway."

"But writers all speak about the South being tragic. You know—Spanish señoritas, black hair and daggers an' haunting music."

He shook his head.

"No, the Northern races are the tragic races—they don't indulge in the cheering luxury of tears."

105 Sally Carrol thought of her graveyard. She supposed that that was vaguely what she had meant when she said it didn't depress her.

"The Italians are about the gayest people in the world—but it's a dull subject," he broke off. "Anyway, I want to tell you you're marrying a pretty fine man."

Sally Carrol was moved by an impulse of confidence.

"I know. I'm the sort of person who wants to be taken care of after a certain point, and I feel sure I will be."

"Shall we dance? You know," he continued as they rose, "it's encouraging to find a girl who knows what she's marrying for. Nine-tenths of them think of it as a sort of walking into a moving-picture sunset."

110   She laughed, and liked him immensely.

Two hours later on the way home she nestled near Harry in the back seat.

"Oh, Harry," she whispered, "it's so co-old!"

"But it's warm in here, darling girl."

"But outside it's cold; and oh, that howling wind!"

115   She buried her face deep in his fur coat and trembled involuntarily as his cold lips kissed the tip of her ear.

IV

THE FIRST WEEK of her visit passed in a whirl. She had her promised toboggan-ride at the back of an automobile through a chill January twilight. Swathed in furs she put in a morning tobogganing on the country-club hill; even tried skiing, to sail through the air for a glorious moment and then land in a tangled laughing bundle on a soft snowdrift. She liked all the winter sports, except an afternoon spent snow-shoeing over a glaring plain under pale yellow sunshine, but she soon realized that these things were for children—that she was being humored and that the enjoyment round her was only a reflection of her own.

At first the Bellamy family puzzled her. The men were reliable and she liked them; to Mr. Bellamy especially, with his iron-gray hair and energetic dignity, she took an immediate fancy, once she found that he was born in Kentucky; this made of him a link between the old life and the new. But toward the women she felt a definite hostility.

Myra, her future sister-in-law, seemed the essence of spiritless conventionality. Her conversation was so utterly devoid of personality that Sally Carrol, who came from a country where a certain amount of charm and assurance could be taken for granted in the women, was inclined to despise her.

"If those women aren't beautiful," she thought, "they're nothing. They just fade out when you look at them. They're glorified domestics. Men are the centre of every mixed group."

Lastly there was Mrs. Bellamy, whom Sally Carrol detested. The first day's impression of an egg had been confirmed—an egg with a cracked, veiny voice and such an ungracious dumpiness of carriage that Sally Carrol felt that if she once fell she would surely scramble. In addition, Mrs. Bellamy seemed to typify the town in being innately hostile to strangers. She called Sally Carrol "Sally," and could not be persuaded that the double name was anything more than a tedious ridiculous nickname. To Sally Carrol this shortening of her name was like presenting her to the public half clothed. She loved "Sally Carrol"; she loathed "Sally." She knew also that Harry's mother disapproved of her bobbed hair; and she had never dared smoke down-stairs after that first day when Mrs. Bellamy had come into the library sniffing violently.

5   Of all the men she met she preferred Roger Patton, who was a frequent visitor at the house. He never again alluded to the Ibsenesque tendency of the populace, but when he came in one day and found her curled upon the sofa bent over "Peer Gynt" he laughed and told her to forget what he'd said—that it was all rot.

And then one afternoon in her second week she and Harry hovered on the edge of a dangerously steep quarrel. She considered that he precipitated it entirely, though the Serbia in the case was an unknown man who had not had his trousers pressed.

They had been walking homeward between mounds of high-piled snow and under a sun which

The allusion is to "Peer Gynt," a play by Ibsen. Fitzgerald may be pointing to a resemblance between Sally Carrol and the play's title character. Both go through frightening odysseys to find out where they belong, and they both play roles that differ from who they really are. Near the end of the play, Peer is accused by the "Button-Moulder" of never having been "himself," and in part III, Sally Carrol has the feeling that, when she is trying to fit into Harry's world, she is "acting a part."

Fitzgerald is alluding to the 1914 assassination of an Austrian Archduke by a Serbian terrorist, causing Austria to declare war on Serbia, which eventually led to World War I.

Sally Carrol scarcely recognized. They passed a little girl done up in gray wool until she resembled a small Teddy bear, and Sally Carrol could not resist a gasp of maternal appreciation.

"Look! Harry!"

"What?"

10   "That little girl—did you see her face?"

"Yes, why?"

"It was red as a little strawberry. Oh, she was cute!"

"Why, your own face is almost as red as that already! Everybody's healthy here. We're out in the cold as soon as we're old enough to walk. Wonderful climate!"

She looked at him and had to agree. He was mighty healthy-looking; so was his brother. And she had noticed the new red in her own cheeks that very morning.

15   Suddenly their glances were caught and held, and they stared for a moment at the street-corner ahead of them. A man was standing there, his knees bent, his eyes gazing upward with a tense expression as though he were about to make a leap toward the chilly sky. And then they both exploded into a shout of laughter, for coming closer they discovered it had been a ludicrous momentary illusion produced by the extreme bagginess of the man's trousers.

"Reckon that's one on us," she laughed.

"He must be a Southerner, judging by those trousers," suggested Harry mischievously.

"Why, Harry!"

Her surprised look must have irritated him.

20   "Those damn Southerners!"

Sally Carrol's eyes flashed.

"Don't call 'em that!"

"I'm sorry, dear," said Harry, malignantly apologetic, "but you know what I think of them. They're sort of—sort of degenerates—not at all like the old Southerners. They've lived so long down there with all the colored people that they've gotten lazy and shiftless."

"Hush your mouth, Harry!" she cried angrily.

25   "They're not! They may be lazy—anybody would be in that climate—but they're my best friends, an' I don't want to hear 'em criticised in any such sweepin' way. Some of 'em are the finest men in the world."

"Oh, I know. They're all right when they come North to college, but of all the hangdog, ill-dressed, slovenly lot I ever saw, a hunch of small-town Southerners are the worst!"

Sally Carrol was clinching her gloved hands and biting her lip furiously.

"Why," continued Harry, "there was one in my class at New Haven, and we all thought that at last we'd found the true type of Southern aristocrat, but it turned out that he wasn't an aristocrat at all —just the son of a Northern carpetbagger, who owned about all the cotton round Mobile."

"A Southerner wouldn't talk the way you're talking now," she said evenly.

15   "They haven't the energy!"

"Or the somethin' else."

"I'm sorry, Sally Carrol, but I've heard you say yourself that you'd never marry—"

"That's quite different. I told you I wouldn't want to tie my life to any of the boys that are round Tarleton now, but I never made any sweepin' generalities."

They walked along in silence.

35   "I probably spread it on a bit thick, Sally Carrol. I'm sorry."

She nodded but made no answer. Five minutes later as they stood in the hallway she suddenly threw her arms round him.

"Oh, Harry," she cried, her eyes brimming with tears, "let's get married next week. I'm afraid of having fusses like that. I'm afraid, Harry. It wouldn't be that way if we were married."

But Harry, being in the wrong, was still irritated.

"That'd be idiotic. We decided on March."

40   The tears in Sally Carrol's eyes faded; her expression hardened slightly.

"Very well—I suppose I shouldn't have said that."
Harry melted.

"Dear little nut!" he cried. "Come and kiss me and let's forget."

That very night at the end of a **vaudeville** performance the orchestra played "Dixie" and Sally Carrol felt something stronger and more enduring than her tears and smiles of the day brim up inside her. She leaned forward gripping the arms of her chair until her face grew crimson.

Vaudeville: a form of live entertainment popular until the early twentieth century

45 "Sort of get you, dear?" whispered Harry.

But she did not hear him. To the spirited throb of the violins and the inspiring beat of the kettledrums her own old ghosts were marching by and on into the darkness, and as **fifes** whistled and sighed in the low encore they seemed so nearly out of sight that she could have waved good-by.

Fifes: small flutes

"Away, Away,
Away down South in Dixie!
Away, away,
Away down South in Dixie!"

V

IT WAS A PARTICULARLY cold night. A sudden thaw had nearly cleared the streets the day before, but now they were traversed again with a powdery wraith of loose snow that travelled in wavy lines before the feet of the wind, and filled the lower air with a fine-particled mist. There was no sky—only a dark, ominous tent that draped in the tops of the streets and was in reality a vast approaching army of snowflakes—while over it all, chilling away the comfort from the brown-and-green glow of lighted windows and muffling the steady trot of the horse pulling their sleigh, interminably washed the north wind. It was a dismal town after all, she thought—dismal.

Sometimes at night it had seemed to her as though no one lived here—they had all gone long ago—leaving lighted houses to be covered in time by tombing heaps of sleet. Oh, if there should be snow on her grave! To be beneath great piles of it all winter long, where even her headstone would be a light shadow against light shadows. Her grave—a grave that should be flower-strewn and washed with sun and rain.

She thought again of those isolated country houses that her train had passed, and of the life there the long winter through—the ceaseless glare through the windows, the crust forming on the soft drifts of snow, finally the slow, cheerless melting, and the harsh spring of which Roger Patton had told her. Her spring—to lose it forever—with its lilacs and the lazy sweetness it stirred in her heart. She was laying away that spring—afterward she would lay away that sweetness.

With a gradual insistence the storm broke. Sally Carrol felt a film of flakes melt quickly on her eyelashes, and Harry reached over a furry arm and drew down her complicated flannel cap. Then the small flakes came in skirmish-line, and the horse bent his neck patiently as a transparency of white appeared momentarily on his coat.

5   "Oh, he's cold, Harry," she said quickly.

"Who? The horse? Oh, no, he isn't. He likes it!"

After another ten minutes they turned a corner and came in sight of their destination. On a tall hill outlined in vivid glaring green against the wintry sky stood the ice palace. It was three stories in the air, with battlements and **embrasures** and narrow icicled windows, and the innumerable electric lights inside made a gorgeous transparency of the great central hall. Sally Carrol clutched Harry's hand under the fur robe.

Embrasures: openings to put the barrel of a gun through

"It's beautiful!" he cried excitedly. "My golly, it's beautiful, isn't it! They haven't had one here since eighty-five!"

Somehow the notion of there not having been one since eighty-five oppressed her. Ice was a ghost, and this mansion of it was surely peopled by those shades of the eighties, with pale faces and blurred snow-filled hair.

10   "Come on, dear," said Harry.

She followed him out of the sleigh and waited while he hitched the horse. A party of four—Gordon, Myra, Roger Patton, and another girl—drew up beside them with a mighty jingle of bells. There were quite a crowd already, bundled in fur or sheepskin, shouting and calling to each other as they moved through the snow, which was now so thick that people could scarcely be distinguished a few yards away.

"It's a hundred and seventy feet tall," Harry was saying to a muffled figure beside him as they trudged toward the entrance; "covers six thousand square yards."

She caught snatches of conversation: "One main hall"—"walls twenty to forty inches thick"—"and the ice cave has almost a mile of—" "this Canuck who built it—"

They found their way inside, and dazed by the magic of the great crystal walls Sally Carrol found herself repeating over and over two lines from "Kubla Khan":

15   "It was a miracle of rare device,
        A sunny pleasure-dome with caves of ice!"

In the great glittering cavern with the dark shut out she took a seat on a wooden bench, and the evening's oppression lifted. Harry was right—it was beautiful; and her gaze travelled the smooth surface of the walls, the blocks for which had been selected for their purity and clearness to obtain this **opalescent**, translucent effect.

"Look! Here we go—oh, boy!" cried Harry.

A band in a far corner struck up "Hail, Hail, the Gang's All Here!" which echoed over to them in wild muddled acoustics, and then the lights suddenly went out; silence seemed to flow down the icy sides and sweep over them. Sally Carrol could still see her white breath in the darkness, and a dim row of pale faces over on the other side.

The music eased to a sighing complaint, and from outside drifted in the full-throated resonant chant of the marching clubs. It grew louder like some **paean** of a viking tribe traversing an ancient

Sally Carrol recalls two lines from Samuel Taylor Coleridge's poem "Kubla Khan," showing her fascination with the ice palace. However, slightly earlier in the poem, Coleridge writes, "Kubla heard from afar/Ancestral voices prophesying war!" And later in the poem, he includes these ominous lines: "That sunny dome! those caves of ice!/ And all who heard should see them there,/And all should cry, Beware! Beware!"

Opalescent: shining like a precious stone called an opal

Paean: a song

Mackinawed: similar to a thick, short wool coat

Luridly: glaringly

Platoon: a group with a common cause

Phantasmagoria: a dreamlike scene of shifting, fantastic, images

wild; it swelled—they were coming nearer; then a row of torches appeared, and another and another, and keeping time with their moccasined feet a long column of gray-**mackinawed** figures swept in, snowshoes slung at their shoulders, torches soaring and flickering as their voices rose along the great walls.

20   The gray column ended and another followed, the light streaming **luridly** this time over red toboggan caps and flaming crimson mackinaws, and as they entered they took up the refrain; then came a long **platoon** of blue and white, of green, of white, of brown and yellow.

"Those white ones are the Wacouta Club," whispered Harry eagerly. "Those are the men you've met round at dances."

The volume of the voices grew; the great cavern was a **phantasmagoria** of torches waving in great banks of fire, of colors and the rhythm of soft-leather steps. The leading column turned and halted, platoon deployed in front of platoon until the whole procession made a solid flag of flame, and then from thousands of voices burst a mighty shout that filled the air like a crash of thunder, and sent the torches wavering. It was magnificent, it was tremendous! To Sally Carrol it was the North offering sacrifice on some mighty altar to the gray pagan God of Snow. As the shout died the band struck up again and there came more singing, and then long reverberating cheers by each club. She sat very quiet listening while the staccato cries rent the stillness; and then she started, for there was a volley of explosion, and great clouds of smoke went up here and there through the cavern—the flash-light photographers at work—and the council was over. With the band at their head the clubs formed in column once more, took up their chant, and began to march out.

"Come on!" shouted Harry. "We want to see the labyrinths down-stairs before they turn the lights off!"

They all rose and started toward the chute— Harry and Sally Carrol in the lead, her little mitten buried in his big fur **gantlet**. At the bottom of the chute was a long empty room of ice, with the ceiling so low that they had to stoop—and their hands were parted. Before she realized what he intended Harry had darted down one of the half-dozen glittering passages that opened into the room and was only a vague receding blot against the green shimmer.

Gantlet: a thick glove

25   "Harry!" she called.

"Come on!" he cried back.

She looked round the empty chamber; the rest of the party had evidently decided to go home, were already outside somewhere in the blundering snow. She hesitated and then darted in after Harry.

"Harry!" she shouted.

She had reached a turning-point thirty feet down; she heard a faint muffled answer far to the left, and with a touch of panic fled toward it. She passed another turning, two more yawning alleys.

30   "Harry!"

No answer. She started to run straight forward, and then turned like lightning and sped back the way she had come, enveloped in a sudden icy terror.

She reached a turn—was it here?—took the left and came to what should have been the outlet into the long, low room, but it was only another glittering passage with darkness at the end. She called again, but the walls gave back a flat, lifeless echo with no reverberations. Retracing her steps she turned another corner, this time following a wide passage. It was like the green lane between the parted waters of the Red Sea, like a damp vault connecting empty tombs.

She slipped a little now as she walked, for ice had formed on the bottom of her overshoes; she had to run her gloves along the half-slippery, half-sticky walls to keep her balance.

"Harry!"

35   Still no answer. The sound she made bounced mockingly down to the end of the passage.

Then on an instant the lights went out, and she was in complete darkness. She gave a small, frightened cry, and sank down into a cold little heap on the ice. She felt her left knee do something as she fell, but she scarcely noticed it as some deep terror far greater than any fear of being lost settled upon her. She was alone with this presence that came out of the North, the dreary loneliness that rose from ice-bound whalers in the Arctic seas, from smokeless, trackless wastes where were strewn the whitened bones of adventure. It was an icy breath of death; it was rolling down low across the land to clutch at her.

With a furious, despairing energy she rose again and started blindly down the darkness. She must get out. She might be lost in here for days, freeze to death and lie embedded in the ice like corpses she had read of, kept perfectly preserved until the melting of a glacier. Harry probably thought she had left with the others—he had gone by now; no one would know until late next day. She reached pitifully for the wall. Forty inches thick, they had said—forty inches thick!

"Oh!"

On both sides of her along the walls she felt things creeping, damp souls that haunted this palace, this town, this North.

40   "Oh, send somebody—send somebody!" she cried aloud.

Clark Darrow—he would understand; or Joe Ewing; she couldn't be left here to wander forever —to be frozen, heart, body, and soul. This her—this Sally Carrol! Why, she was a happy thing. She was a happy little girl. She liked warmth and summer and Dixie. These things were foreign—foreign.

"You're not crying," something said aloud.

"You'll never cry any more. Your tears would just freeze; all tears freeze up here!"

She sprawled full length on the ice.

45   "Oh, God!" she faltered.

A long single file of minutes went by, and with a great weariness she felt her eyes closing. Then some one seemed to sit down near here and take her face in warm, soft hands. She looked up gratefully.

"Why, it's Margery Lee," she crooned softly to herself. "I knew you'd come." It really was Margery

Lee, and she was just as Sally Carrol had known she would be, with a young, white brow, and wide, welcoming eyes, and a hoop-skirt of some soft material that was quite comforting to rest on.

"Margery Lee."

It was getting darker now and darker—all those tombstones ought to be repainted, sure enough, only that would spoil 'em, of course. Still, you ought to be able to see 'em.

50   Then after a succession of moments that went fast and then slow, but seemed to be ultimately resolving themselves into a multitude of blurred rays converging toward a pale-yellow sun, she heard a great cracking noise break her new-found stillness.

It was the sun, it was a light; a torch, and a torch beyond that, and another one, and voices; a face took flesh below the torch, heavy arms raised her, and she felt something on her cheek—it felt wet. Some one had seized her and was rubbing her face with snow. How ridiculous—with snow!

"Sally Carrol! Sally Carrol!"

It was Dangerous Dan McGrew; and two other faces she didn't know.

"Child, child! We've been looking for you two hours! Harry's half-crazy!"

55   Things came rushing back into place—the singing, the torches, the great shout of the marching clubs. She squirmed in Patton's arms and gave a long low cry.

"Oh, I want to get out of here! I'm going back home. Take me home"—her voice rose to a scream that sent a chill to Harry's heart as he came racing down the next passage—"to-morrow!" she cried with delirious, unrestrained passion—"To-morrow! To-morrow! To-morrow!"

VI

THE WEALTH OF golden sunlight poured a quite enervating yet oddly comforting heat over the house where day long it faced the dusty stretch of road. Two birds were making a great to-do in a cool spot found among the branches of a tree next door, and down the street a colored woman was announcing herself melodiously as a purveyor of strawberries. It was April afternoon.

Sally Carrol Happer, resting her chin on her arm, and her arm on an old window-seat, gazed sleepily down over the spangled dust whence the heat waves were rising for the first time this spring. She was watching a very ancient Ford turn a perilous corner and rattle and groan to a jolting stop at the end of the walls. She made no sound, and in a minute a strident familiar whistle rent the air. Sally Carrol smiled and blinked.

"Good mawnin'."

A head appeared tortuously from under the cartop below.

5   " 'Tain't mawnin'."

"Sure enough!" she said in affected surprise. "I guess maybe not."

"What you doin'?"

"Eatin' green peach. 'Spect to die any minute."

Clark twisted himself a last impossible notch to get a view of her face.

10   "Water's warm as a kettla steam, Sally Carrol. Wanta go swimmin'?"

"Hate to move," sighed Sally Carrol lazily, "but I reckon so."

QUESTIONS

1. What are the meanings and connotations of F. Scott Fitzgerald's language in paragraph 1? How does this description impact the tone?

2. The author humorously characterizes the protagonist, Sally Carrol, in paragraphs 3 and 14. How does this description potentially impact a reader's opinion of her?

3. What can you infer from the description of the town in paragraph 21?

4. In paragraphs 61 and 62, Sally Carrol's personality is more fully developed. How do the new additions change our first impressions?

5. At the beginning of part II, Fitzgerald introduces yet another side of Sally Carrol when she enjoys visiting the cemetery, "one of her favorite haunts," with Harry. What do you think she means when she remarks that one of the dead, Margery Lee, was "nice" to have "died when she was twenty-nine"?

6. When Sally Carrol is imagining what Margery Lee may have been like, what does her description (in paragraphs 12 and 14 of part II) say about her concept of herself and her heritage?

7. Analyze how the language in part II, paragraphs 37 and 38, impacts the tone and meaning.

8. The contrasts between part II and part III are powerful and stark. Why is this seeming lack of transition more effective than a traditional or gradual change?

9. The word choices in the first paragraphs of part III emphasize the discomfort Sally Carrol is enduring. List some words that are directly related to the cold and discuss how they impact the tone and meaning.

10. When Sally Carrol wants to go sledding, Harry says, "That's for kids." Later, in paragraph 31 of part III, Sally Carrol feels "as though she had been unjustly spanked...." When she asks to help two boys building a snowman, Harry says, "You dream!" What can you infer from these events and statements?

11. In part III, paragraph 19, Sally Carrol compares the library of Harry's family to that of her own family. What are some of the word choices that imply her distaste for where she is and her preference for where she came from? What is the impact of the connotations of the words?

12. What can you infer from Sally Carrol's statement that she occasionally looks out the window and imagines that "a flurry of snow...[is]...just as if somethin' dead was movin' " (part III, paragraph 75)?

13. What is being discussed in part III, paragraphs 108 and 109? How do the connotations of the word choices fit in with what is already known about Sally Carrol and help you fully understand the relationship between her and Harry?

14. What can be inferred from the last paragraph of part III?

15. In part IV, paragraph 4, Fitzgerald sums up Sally Carrol's feelings about Harry's mother, Mrs. Bellamy. What is the impact of this passage on the meaning and tone?

16. The quarrel that Harry starts in part IV, paragraph 17 is a flashpoint that directly relates to the North versus South element in the story. What is another theme that more directly involves Harry and Sally Carrol's relationship? Explain how these two themes work together.

17. How does the abrupt jump between parts IV and V change the tone and contribute to the impact of "The Ice Palace"?

18. Examine paragraph 2 of part V. What are the meanings and connotations that can be derived from the author's word choices? How do they impact the tone?

19. Soon afterward, in paragraph 9, the ghost motif reappears as Sally Carrol thinks of the ice palace being "peopled by...shades...with pale faces and blurred snow-filled hair." How does this choice of words act as foreshadowing?

20. In part V, paragraph 36, Fitzgerald's language describes Sally Carrol's horror after getting lost. Analyze the second half of the paragraph, beginning with "She was alone...." How do the text and its connotations impact the meaning and tone?

21. What inferences can be drawn from Sally Carrol's nightmarish vision in paragraphs 40-48? What makes the word choices effective?

22. Compare and contrast the opening few paragraphs of parts I and VI, focusing on the parallelism and important differences in word choice. How does this structure contribute to the story's overall impact?

Ambrose Bierce

An Occurrence at Owl Creek Bridge

INTRODUCTION

An Occurrence at Owl Creek Bridge

Bierce's colorful and richly detailed story of the hanging of a quickly convicted Confederate saboteur during the Civil War was originally published on July 13, 1890, in the *San Francisco Examiner*, a newspaper, for which Bierce was a staff writer. Soon, he included it in what many critics consider his best book, *Tales of Soldiers and Civilians* (1891). Bierce had served with distinction in the Union army, participating in several well-known battles, such as Shiloh in Tennessee, which occurred near the actual Owl Creek. During one battle, he was seriously wounded in the head. After being hospitalized for a few months, he returned to duty, but suffered from blackouts, which led him to accept a medical discharge from the army in early 1865. These periods of blacking out might have furnished some of the basis and imagery for "An Occurrence at Owl Creek Bridge."

Ambrose Bierce

Although Bierce is now known primarily for his Civil War stories and his bitingly satirical and often hilarious *Devil's Dictionary* (1906), he also had a successful writing career as a contributor of essays and humorous articles to various California publications and worked as a staffer at the San Francisco-based *News-Letter and California Advertiser*. There he wrote popular pieces that were collected in his first book, *The Fiend's Delight* (1872), and a second book, *Nuggets and Dust* (1873). These collections made him a national celebrity and earned him laudatory comparisons to Mark Twain, who had become an acquaintance. Bierce would go on to write for other papers, publish several more books, and become one of the leading American humorists and short story writers during the late nineteenth and early twentieth centuries.

Bierce was born June 24, 1842, near Horse Cave Creek in Ohio, about a hundred miles southeast of the capital city of Columbus. He was one of thirteen children, and his father had a large library where Bierce supplemented his education. Not much, however, is known about his early childhood and schooling. During the Civil War, he worked as a mapmaker and engineer, though he also took part in some heavy combat, rising steadily up the ranks to first lieutenant. After his discharge, he was given an honorary promotion to major.

Like many young men of his time, Bierce went to California seeking a new life and soon started his writing career in San Francisco. After marrying in 1871, and spending a few years in London, he and his family returned to San Francisco.

Bierce continued his successful writing career, began working for William Randolph Hearst in 1877 at the *San Francisco Examiner*, and produced the bulk of his most impressive writing over the next 20 years including several collections of stories that sold very well. But in 1889, his son was killed in a gunfight, in 1901, his other son died of pneumonia, and in 1904, after years of strife, his wife filed for divorce.

In 1912, Bierce left the U.S. for Mexico. He had been supportive of Pancho Villa's pro-democracy rebellion, and in 1913, on the day after Christmas, he wrote his daughter a letter, which was sent from Chihuahua, Villa's headquarters. Then, Bierce mysteriously disappeared. Many believe that he died fighting with Villa's forces in 1914, but there has never been any solid evidence for that or any of the other theories about his death.

An Occurrence at Owl Creek Bridge
Ambrose Bierce (1891)

I

A MAN STOOD UPON a railroad bridge in northern Alabama, looking down into the swift water twenty feet below. The man's hands were behind his back, the wrists bound with a cord. A rope closely encircled his neck. It was attached to a stout cross-timber above his head and the slack fell to the level of his knees. Some loose boards laid upon the ties supporting the rails of the railway supplied a footing for him and his executioners—two private soldiers of the Federal army, directed by a sergeant who in civil life may have been a deputy sheriff. At a short remove upon the same temporary platform was an officer in the uniform of his rank, armed. He was a captain. A sentinel at each end of the bridge stood with his rifle in the position known as "support," that is to say, vertical in front of the left shoulder, the hammer resting on the forearm thrown straight across the chest—a formal and unnatural position, enforcing an erect carriage of the body. It did not appear to be the duty of these two men to know what was occurring at the center of the bridge; they merely blockaded the two ends of the foot planking that traversed it.

Beyond one of the sentinels nobody was in sight; the railroad ran straight away into a forest for a hundred yards, then, curving, was lost to view. Doubtless there was an outpost farther along. The other bank of the stream was open ground—a gentle slope topped with a stockade of vertical tree trunks, loopholed for rifles, with a single **embrasure** through which protruded the muzzle of a brass cannon commanding the bridge. Midway up the slope between the bridge and fort were the spectators—a single company of infantry in line, at "parade rest," the butts of their rifles on the ground, the barrels inclining slightly backward against the right shoulder, the hands crossed upon the stock. A lieutenant stood at the right of the line, the point of his sword

Embrasure: an opening in a fortification used for the placing of the barrel of a weapon

upon the ground, his left hand resting upon his right. Excepting the group of four at the center of the bridge, not a man moved. The company faced the bridge, staring stonily, motionless. The sentinels, facing the banks of the stream, might have been statues to adorn the bridge. The captain stood with folded arms, silent, observing the work of his subordinates, but making no sign. Death is a dignitary who when he comes announced is to be received with formal manifestations of respect, even by those most familiar with him. In the code of military etiquette silence and fixity are forms of deference.

The man who was engaged in being hanged was apparently about thirty-five years of age. He was a civilian, if one might judge from his habit, which was that of a planter. His features were good—a straight nose, firm mouth, broad forehead, from which his long, dark hair was combed straight back, falling behind his ears to the collar of his well fitting frock coat. He wore a moustache and pointed beard, but no whiskers; his eyes were large and dark gray, and had a kindly expression which one would hardly have expected in one whose neck was in the hemp. Evidently this was no vulgar assassin. The liberal military code makes provision for hanging many kinds of persons, and gentlemen are not excluded.

The preparations being complete, the two private soldiers stepped aside and each drew away the plank upon which he had been standing. The sergeant turned to the captain, saluted and placed himself immediately behind that officer, who in turn moved apart one pace. These movements left the condemned man and the sergeant standing on the two ends of the same plank, which spanned three of the cross-ties of the bridge. The end upon which the civilian stood almost, but not quite, reached a fourth. This plank had been held in place by the weight of the captain; it was now held by that of the sergeant. At a signal from the former the latter would step aside, the plank would tilt and the condemned man go down between two ties. The arrangement commended itself to his judgement as simple and effective. His face had not been covered nor his eyes bandaged. He looked a moment at his "unsteadfast footing," then let his gaze wander to the swirling water of the stream racing madly beneath his feet. A piece of dancing driftwood caught his attention and his eyes followed it down the current. How slowly it appeared to move! What a sluggish stream!

5   He closed his eyes in order to fix his last thoughts upon his wife and children. The water, touched to gold by the early sun, the brooding mists under the banks at some distance down the stream, the fort, the soldiers, the piece of drift—all had distracted him. And now he became conscious of a new disturbance. Striking through the thought of his dear ones was sound which he could neither ignore nor understand, a sharp, distinct, metallic percussion like the stroke of a blacksmith's hammer upon the anvil; it had the same ringing quality. He wondered what it was, and whether immeasurably distant or near by—it seemed both. Its recurrence was regular, but as slow as the tolling of a death knell. He awaited each new stroke with impatience and—he knew not why—apprehension. The intervals of silence grew progressively longer; the delays became maddening. With their greater infrequency the sounds increased in strength and sharpness. They hurt his ear like the trust of a knife; he feared he would shriek. What he heard was the ticking of his watch.

He unclosed his eyes and saw again the water below him. "If I could free my hands," he thought, "I might throw off the noose and spring into the stream. By diving I could evade the bullets and, swimming vigorously, reach the bank, take to the woods and get away home. My home, thank God, is as yet outside their lines; my wife and little ones are still beyond the invader's farthest advance."

As these thoughts, which have here to be set down in words, were flashed into the doomed man's brain rather than evolved from it the captain nodded to the sergeant. The sergeant stepped aside.

II

PEYTON FARQUHAR WAS a well to do planter, of an old and highly respected Alabama family. Being a slave owner and like other slave owners a politician, he was naturally an original **secessionist** and ardently devoted to the Southern cause. Circumstances of an imperious nature, which it is unnecessary to relate here, had prevented him from taking service with that gallant army which had fought the disastrous campaigns ending with the fall of Corinth, and he chafed under the inglorious restraint, longing for the release of his energies, the larger life of the soldier, the opportunity for distinction. That opportunity, he felt, would come, as it comes to all in wartime. Meanwhile he did what he could. No service was too humble for him to perform in the aid of the South, no adventure too perilous for him to undertake if consistent with the character of a civilian who was at heart a soldier, and who in good faith and without too much qualification assented to at least a part of the frankly villainous dictum that all is fair in love and war.

Secessionist: one who believed in leaving (seceding) from the United States, as the Confederate states did

"The fall of Corinth" alludes to an important victory for the North, gaining control of a railhead in Corinth, Mississippi, on October 4, 1862. Ambrose Bierce fought for the Union in the battle of Corinth.

One evening while Farquhar and his wife were sitting on a rustic bench near the entrance to his grounds, a gray-clad soldier rode up to the gate and asked for a drink of water. Mrs. Farquhar was only too happy to serve him with her own white hands. While she was fetching the water her husband approached the dusty horseman and inquired eagerly for news from the front.

"The Yanks are repairing the railroads," said the man, "and are getting ready for another advance. They have reached the Owl Creek bridge, put it in order and built a stockade on the north bank. The commandant has issued an order, which is posted everywhere, declaring that any civilian caught interfering with the railroad, its bridges, tunnels, or trains will be **summarily** hanged. I saw the order."

"How far is it to the Owl Creek bridge?" Farquhar asked.

5   "About thirty miles."

"Is there no force on this side of the creek?"

Summarily: quickly without formalities, in this case without a trial

"Only a picket post half a mile out, on the railroad, and a single sentinel at this end of the bridge."

"Suppose a man—a civilian and student of hanging—should elude the picket post and perhaps get the better of the sentinel," said Farquhar, smiling, "what could he accomplish?"

The soldier reflected. "I was there a month ago," he replied. "I observed that the flood of last winter had lodged a great quantity of driftwood against the wooden pier at this end of the bridge. It is now dry and would burn like tinder."

10   The lady had now brought the water, which the soldier drank. He thanked her ceremoniously, bowed to her husband and rode away. An hour later, after nightfall, he repassed the plantation, going northward in the direction from which he had come. He was a Federal scout.

III

AS PEYTON FARQUHAR FELL straight downward through the bridge he lost consciousness and was as one already dead. From this state he was awakened— ages later, it seemed to him—by the pain of a sharp pressure upon his throat, followed by a sense of suffocation. Keen, **poignant** agonies seemed to shoot from his neck downward through every fiber of his body and limbs. These pains appeared to flash along well defined lines of **ramification** and to beat with an inconceivably rapid periodicity. They seemed like streams of pulsating fire heating him to an intolerable temperature. As to his head, he was conscious of nothing but a feeling of fullness—of congestion. These sensations were unaccompanied by thought. The intellectual part of his nature was already **effaced**; he had power only to feel, and feeling was torment. He was conscious of motion. Encompassed in a luminous cloud, of which he was now merely the fiery heart, without material substance, he swung through unthinkable arcs of oscillation, like a vast pendulum. Then all

Poignant: deep and powerful

Ramification: a result of an event

Effaced: erased

at once, with terrible suddenness, the light about him shot upward with the noise of a loud splash; a frightful roaring was in his ears, and all was cold and dark. The power of thought was restored; he knew that the rope had broken and he had fallen into the stream. There was no additional strangulation; the noose about his neck was already suffocating him and kept the water from his lungs. To die of hanging at the bottom of a river!—the idea seemed to him ludicrous. He opened his eyes in the darkness and saw above him a gleam of light, but how distant, how inaccessible! He was still sinking, for the light became fainter and fainter until it was a mere glimmer. Then it began to grow and brighten, and he knew that he was rising toward the surface—knew it with reluctance, for he was now very comfortable. "To be hanged and drowned," he thought, "that is not so bad; but I do not wish to be shot. No; I will not be shot; that is not fair."

He was not conscious of an effort, but a sharp pain in his wrist apprised him that he was trying to free his hands. He gave the struggle his attention, as an idler might observe the feat of a juggler, without interest in the outcome. What splendid effort!— what magnificent, what superhuman strength! Ah, that was a fine endeavor! Bravo! The cord fell away; his arms parted and floated upward, the hands dimly seen on each side in the growing light. He watched them with a new interest as first one and then the other pounced upon the noose at his neck. They tore it away and thrust it fiercely aside, its **undulations** resembling those of a water snake. "Put it back, put it back!" He thought he shouted these words to his hands, for the undoing of the noose had been succeeded by the direst pang that he had yet experienced. His neck ached horribly; his brain was on fire, his heart, which had been fluttering faintly, gave a great leap, trying to force itself out at his mouth. His whole body was racked and wrenched with an insupportable anguish! But his disobedient hands gave no heed to the command. They beat the water vigorously with quick, downward strokes,

Undulations: regular wave movements from side to side

forcing him to the surface. He felt his head emerge; his eyes were blinded by the sunlight; his chest expanded convulsively, and with a supreme and crowning agony his lungs engulfed a great draught of air, which instantly he expelled in a shriek!

Preternaturally: abnormally, beyond the natural

He was now in full possession of his physical senses. They were, indeed, **preternaturally** keen and alert. Something in the awful disturbance of his organic system had so exalted and refined them that they made record of things never before perceived. He felt the ripples upon his face and heard their separate sounds as they struck. He looked at the forest on the bank of the stream, saw the individual trees, the leaves and the veining of each leaf—he saw the very insects upon them: the locusts, the brilliant bodied flies, the gray spiders stretching their webs from twig to twig. He noted the prismatic colors in all the dewdrops upon a million blades of grass. The humming of the gnats that danced above the eddies of the stream, the beating of the dragon flies' wings, the strokes of the water spiders' legs, like oars which had lifted their boat—all these made audible music. A fish slid along beneath his eyes and he heard the rush of its body parting the water.

He had come to the surface facing down the stream; in a moment the visible world seemed to wheel slowly round, himself the pivotal point, and he saw the bridge, the fort, the soldiers upon the bridge, the captain, the sergeant, the two privates, his executioners. They were in silhouette against the blue sky. They shouted and **gesticulated**, pointing at him. The captain had drawn his pistol, but did not fire; the others were unarmed. Their movements were grotesque and horrible, their forms gigantic.

Gesticulated: moved one's hands or arms in an exaggerated manner

5   Suddenly he heard a sharp report and something struck the water smartly within a few inches of his head, spattering his face with spray. He heard a second report, and saw one of the sentinels with his rifle at his shoulder, a light cloud of blue smoke rising from the muzzle. The man in the water saw the eye of the man on the bridge

gazing into his own through the sights of the rifle. He observed that it was a gray eye and remembered having read that gray eyes were keenest, and that all famous marksmen had them. Nevertheless, this one had missed.

A counter-swirl had caught Farquhar and turned him half round; he was again looking at the forest on the bank opposite the fort. The sound of a clear, high voice in a monotonous singsong now rang out behind him and came across the water with a distinctness that pierced and subdued all other sounds, even the beating of the ripples in his ears. Although no soldier, he had frequented camps enough to know the dread significance of that deliberate, drawling, **aspirated** chant; the lieutenant on shore was taking a part in the morning's work. How coldly and pitilessly— with what an even, calm intonation, presaging, and enforcing tranquility in the men—with what accurately measured interval fell those cruel words:

Aspirated: stated with a strong exhalation of breath

"Company!…Attention!…Shoulder arms!… Ready!…Aim!…Fire!"

Farquhar dived—dived as deeply as he could. The water roared in his ears like the voice of Niagara, yet he heard the dull thunder of the volley and, rising again toward the surface, met shining bits of metal, singularly flattened, **oscillating** slowly downward. Some of them touched him on the face and hands, then fell away, continuing their descent. One lodged between his collar and neck; it was uncomfortably warm and he snatched it out.

Oscillating: moving back and forth at a steady speed

As he rose to the surface, gasping for breath, he saw that he had been a long time under water; he was perceptibly farther downstream—nearer to safety. The soldiers had almost finished reloading; the metal ramrods flashed all at once in the sunshine as they were drawn from the barrels, turned in the air, and thrust into their sockets. The two sentinels fired again, independently and ineffectually.

10 The hunted man saw all this over his shoulder; he was now swimming vigorously with the current.

His brain was as energetic as his arms and legs; he thought with the rapidity of lightning:

"The officer," he reasoned, "will not make that martinet's error a second time. It is as easy to dodge a volley as a single shot. He has probably already given the command to fire at will. God help me, I cannot dodge them all!"

An appalling splash within two yards of him was followed by a loud, rushing sound, **diminuendo**, which seemed to travel back through the air to the fort and died in an explosion which stirred the very river to its deeps! A rising sheet of water curved over him, fell down upon him, blinded him, strangled him! The cannon had taken an hand in the game. As he shook his head free from the commotion of the smitten water he heard the deflected shot humming through the air ahead, and in an instant it was cracking and smashing the branches in the forest beyond.

Diminuendo: a musical term meaning decreasing in volume

"They will not do that again," he thought; "the next time they will use a charge of grape. I must keep my eye upon the gun; the smoke will apprise me—the report arrives too late; it lags behind the missile. That is a good gun."

Suddenly he felt himself whirled round and round—spinning like a top. The water, the banks, the forests, the now distant bridge, fort and men, all were commingled and blurred. Objects were represented by their colors only; circular horizontal streaks of color—that was all he saw. He had been caught in a vortex and was being whirled on with a velocity of advance and gyration that made him giddy and sick. In a few moments he was flung upon the gravel at the foot of the left bank of the stream—the southern bank—and behind a projecting point which concealed him from his enemies. The sudden arrest of his motion, the abrasion of one of his hands on the gravel, restored him, and he wept with delight. He dug his fingers into the sand, threw it over himself in handfuls and audibly blessed it. It looked like diamonds, rubies, emeralds; he could think of nothing beautiful which it did not resemble. The trees upon the bank were giant garden plants; he noted a definite order in their arrangement, inhaled the fragrance of their blooms. A strange roseate light shone through the spaces among their trunks and the wind made in their branches the music of Aeolian harps. He had not wish to perfect his escape—he was content to remain in that enchanting spot until retaken.

An Aeolian harp is an instrument usually made of wood that is played by the force of the wind and is named after Aeolus, the mythological Greek god of wind.

15   A whiz and a rattle of grapeshot among the branches high above his head roused him from his dream. The baffled cannoneer had fired him a random farewell. He sprang to his feet, rushed up the sloping bank, and plunged into the forest.

All that day he traveled, laying his course by the rounding sun. The forest seemed interminable; nowhere did he discover a break in it, not even a woodman's road. He had not known that he lived in so wild a region. There was something uncanny in the revelation.

By nightfall he was fatigued, footsore, famished. The thought of his wife and children urged him on. At last he found a road which led him in what he knew to be the right direction. It was as wide and straight as a city street, yet it seemed untraveled. No fields bordered it, no dwelling anywhere. Not so much as the barking of a dog suggested human habitation. The black bodies of the trees formed a straight wall on both sides, terminating on the horizon in a point, like a diagram in a lesson in perspective. Overhead, as he looked up through this rift in the wood, shone great golden stars looking unfamiliar and grouped in strange constellations. He was sure they were arranged in some order which had a secret and malign significance. The wood on either side was full of singular noises, among which—once, twice, and again—he distinctly heard whispers in an unknown tongue.

His neck was in pain and lifting his hand to it found it horribly swollen. He knew that it had a circle of black where the rope had bruised it. His eyes felt congested; he could no longer close them.

His tongue was swollen with thirst; he relieved its fever by thrusting it forward from between his teeth into the cold air. How softly the turf had carpeted the untraveled avenue—he could no longer feel the roadway beneath his feet!

Doubtless, despite his suffering, he had fallen asleep while walking, for now he sees another scene—perhaps he has merely recovered from a **delirium**. He stands at the gate of his own home. All is as he left it, and all bright and beautiful in the morning sunshine. He must have traveled the entire night. As he pushes open the gate and passes up the wide white walk, he sees a flutter of female garments; his wife, looking fresh and cool and sweet, steps down from the veranda to meet him. At the bottom of the steps she stands waiting, with a smile of ineffable joy, an attitude of matchless grace and dignity. Ah, how beautiful she is! He springs forwards with extended arms. As he is about to clasp her he feels a stunning blow upon the back of the neck; a blinding white light blazes all about him with a sound like the shock of a cannon—then all is darkness and silence!

20   Peyton Farquhar was dead; his body, with a broken neck, swung gently from side to side beneath the timbers of the Owl Creek bridge.

Delirium: confusion and disorientation

QUESTIONS

1. What do the point of view, setting, and writing style at the beginning of the story contribute to the meaning and tone?

2. How does the personification of Death near the end of paragraph 2 change the tone and perspective?

3. Examine the description of the protagonist, "who was engaged in being hanged." What can you infer about what is happening to him?

4. What does the word "liberal" mean in the last sentence of paragraph 3? What are the normal connotations of the word and why do they not apply in this case?

5. In the second half of paragraph 4, the point of view abruptly changes. What is it now, and what is the impact on the meaning and tone?

6. In paragraph 1, the water is "swift," and in paragraph 4 it goes from "swirling" to "racing madly" with a "piece of dancing driftwood" in it. But Farquhar describes it as moving "slowly...a sluggish stream!" What can be inferred from how he sees the water?

7. In paragraph 5, what can be inferred by Farquhar's obsession with the "sharp, distinct, metallic" sounds and the "maddening" delays between them?

8. Notice the unusual word choices in paragraph 7: "these thoughts...were flashed into the doomed man's brain rather than evolved from it." Why might the author choose to use a passive verb to describe the origin of Farquhar's vision of freedom? What is the impact on the meaning and tone?

9. The transition from part I to part II is almost nonexistent, as the narration seems to become a commonplace biographical sketch of the protagonist. What is the one word that is repeated in order to make the transition more effective and sensible? What is the effect of this abrupt change of style?

10. Examine the description of Farquhar. What can you infer from the facts that he was a slave owner and "a civilian who was at heart a soldier" and believed, "at least a part of the frankly villainous dictum that all is fair in love and war"?

11. How do the events and word choices in part II, paragraphs 2 and 3 affect the meaning and tone of this section?

12. In part II, paragraph 8, what can you infer from Farquhar's description of himself as "a civilian and student of hanging," followed by his "smiling" inquiry about what such a man could "accomplish"?

13. Analyze the overall effect of the shocking endings of paragraph 5 in part I and paragraph 10 in part II. What does this structure cause you to expect in the rest of the story?

14. Again, as in the rough transition from part I to II, there is an abrupt change from part II to III, and this time there appears to be no transition at all. How does the structure mirror the content?

15. Determine the meanings of the horrific language in part III, paragraph 1.

16. In part III, paragraph 2, what are the implications of his body trying to free itself as his mind watches "as an idler might observe"?

17. Explain the meanings and connotations of part III, paragraph 13.

18. In paragraphs 16 and 17 of part III, Farquhar notices that the region he lives in is denser and wilder than he remembered it, and he also thinks, "There was something uncanny in the revelation." Then, when he finds a road that leads him in "the right direction," it is a very unusual road: "wide and straight as a city street, yet it seemed untraveled." Above it, the "great golden stars" are "unfamiliar and grouped in strange constellations...in some order which had a secret and malign significance." He also hears "whispers in an unknown tongue." What can be inferred from these observations? What is left uncertain?

19. What does the description of Farquhar in paragraph 18 of part III connote? How are the meaning and tone affected?

20. What are the effects of the point of view and word choices in part III, paragraph 19? Why does the author suddenly shift the majority of tenses from past to present? What is the effect on the meaning and tone?

21. How do the style and word choices in the final paragraph affect the story? Why does the author change back to the past tense, for example?

22. Discuss two major themes in "An Occurrence at Owl Creek Bridge."

Carl Sandburg

Grass

INTRODUCTION

Grass

This poem, one of Sandburg's reactions to the horrors of World War I, is included in his 1918 collection titled *Cornhuskers*, his follow-up to *Chicago Poems* (1916). Most of Sandburg's poetry centers on and celebrates the common American people, their jobs, and their lives, and he often championed causes related to workers' rights and social equality. "Grass," however, is darker and deals with how governments and people in general tend to gloss over the gory details of war, similar to how grass covers the graves of those who fought and died.

Carl Sandburg

Sandburg was born on January 6, 1878, in Galesburg, Illinois. As a young man, he worked at various menial jobs. In 1898, he enlisted in the army during the Spanish-American War and served in Puerto Rico. After he returned home, he attended Lombard College in Galesburg and edited the college journal but never graduated; later in his life, Sandburg would receive honorary degrees from Harvard, Yale, and several other universities.

While Sandburg was working as a journalist in Chicago in 1919, his *Cornhuskers* collection earned him the Poetry Society of America Award, which, in 1922, would be renamed the Pulitzer Prize for Poetry. He also earned a Pulitzer in 1940 for *Abraham Lincoln: The War Years*, the final volume of his highly acclaimed Lincoln biography, and another Pulitzer for his *Complete Poems* in 1951.

Sandburg died on July 22, 1967.

Grass
Carl Sandburg (1918)

Pile the bodies high at Austerlitz and Waterloo,

Shovel them under and let me work—

    I am the grass; I cover all.

And pile them high at Gettysburg

And pile them high at Ypres and Verdun.   **5**

Shovel them under and let me work.

Two years, ten years, and passengers ask the conductor:

    What place is this?

    Where are we now?

    I am the grass.   **10**

    Let me work.

The place names refer to large, well-known battles that caused many deaths. Austerlitz (in Moravia, now the Czech Republic, 1805) and Water-loo (Belgium, 1815) featured the army of Napoleon against various enemies; Gettysburg (Pennsylvania, 1863) was, of course, the major clash of the Civil War; Ypres (in Flanders, now Belgium, 1914, 1915, and 1917) and Verdun (France, 1916) designate several battles in World War I. Because the poem was published in 1918, many readers would have either taken part in or known of others who served in World War I.

QUESTIONS

1. What is the point of view, and what effect does it have on the meaning and tone?

2. What is a logical inference of the poem, based on the personification and the attitude of the grass?

3. Analyze the connotations of the repeated commands "pile them high" and "shovel them under." What are the effects on the tone and meaning?

4. In the second stanza, what can you infer from lines 8-10?

5. This poem is written in free verse, although there is a visible structure, and the repetition emphasizes important ideas. How does the composition of the poem affect its meaning, and impact?

Edna St. Vincent Millay

Sonnet II

INTRODUCTION

Sonnet II

In 1917, Millay published her first book of poetry, *Renascence and Other Poems*, including "Sonnet II," which has become one of the most recognized American poems about the pain of losing a loved one. While her varied and active life was full of romance and many accomplishments, Millay is remembered for her skillful sonnets.

Edna St. Vincent Millay

Edna St. Vincent Millay was born in Rockland, Maine, on February 22, 1892; she wrote traditional verse, but with modern themes. She was also a playwright and short story writer (under the pen name Nancy Boyd). In 1923, she became the third woman to win the Pulitzer Prize for poetry. Raised by a strong, independent mother who divorced Millay's father in 1904, she would, through her literary success, become a powerful voice for feminism. She grew up in Maine, went to school at Vassar, and moved to Greenwich Village after graduation.

Millay's first success came in 1912 when she entered her poem "Renascence" in a poetry contest and won fourth place; the first and second place winners, however, both thought that Millay's poem was the best submission. Her strong feminism and uncompromising lifestyle made her both famous and controversial.

Millay married Eugen Jan Boissevain in 1923; he died in 1949. The following year, Millay suffered a heart attack and died on October 19, at age 58.

Sonnet II
Edna St. Vincent Millay (1918)

Time does not bring relief; you all have lied
    Who told me time would ease me of my pain!
    I miss him in the weeping of the rain;
I want him at the shrinking of the tide;
The old snows melt from every mountain-side,   **5**
    And last year's leaves are smoke in every lane;
    But last year's bitter loving must remain
Heaped on my heart, and my old thoughts abide!

There are a hundred places where I fear
    To go,—so with his memory they brim!   **10**
And entering with relief some quiet place
Where never fell his foot or shone his face
I say, "There is no memory of him here!"
    And so stand stricken, so remembering him!

QUESTIONS

1. Why is the allusion to a cliché effective as an opening sentence? How does this choice of words help set the meaning and tone of the first four lines?

2. Interpret the figurative language in lines 3-5. What do these metaphors have in common, and how do they blend with and strengthen the tone?

3. What do lines 3-4 imply? How does parallelism in these lines impact the poem?

4. How does the comparison of leaves to smoke in line 6 strengthen the tone of grief and the theme of loss?

5. What does the phrase "bitter loving" tell you about the relationship that has ended?

6. How do Millay's word choices in the sestet set up and increase the power of the last line? What is the meaning of lines 9-10?

7. This poem is a traditional Italian sonnet, a form that is relatively rigid. Does this form aesthetically fit the content? How does it impact the tone and meaning?

8. State at least two themes within the poem and analyze how their development and interaction add complexity to the poem.

Edwin Arlington Robinson

Richard Cory

INTRODUCTION

Richard Cory

Robinson's *The Children of the Night* (privately published in 1897; reprinted in 1905) includes "Richard Cory." The title character is a resident of "Tilbury Town," a fictional place that Robinson used as a representation of typical, small-town American culture, especially in New England, around the turn of the century. Most of his well-known poems are set there. "Richard Cory" is, arguably, his most famous poem.

Edwin Arlington Robinson

Edwin Arlington Robinson was one of the first major American poets of the 20th century, due in large part to his attracting the attention and admiration of president Theodore Roosevelt, who encouraged Scribner's to republish *The Children of the Night*. The 1905 edition of the book brought Robinson's name and works to the attention of major magazines and literary critics. In 1922, his *Collected Poems* won him the first of three Pulitzer Prizes.

Born on December 22, 1869, in Head Tide, Maine, he attended Harvard, but his family experienced serious financial problems, causing him to drop out. His father died in 1892, his mother in 1896, and by 1909, both his brothers had also died. Virtually alone and destitute, Robinson, who had moved to New York City, had trouble earning a living and went through a period in which he struggled with alcoholism.

Much of the misfortune in his life is reflected in his poetry, in which many of the characters deal with failure, tragedy, and death. Robinson himself rose above his problems to create a well-respected body of work that is still seen as some of the best poetry in American literature. On April 6, 1935, he died in New York while working on *King Jasper*, his last book.

Richard Cory
Edwin Arlington Robinson (1897)

Whenever Richard Cory went down town,
We people on the pavement looked at him:
He was a gentleman from sole to crown,
Clean favored, and imperially slim.

And he was always quietly arrayed,   5
And he was always human when he talked;
But still he fluttered pulses when he said,
"Good-morning," and he glittered when he walked.

And he was rich—yes, richer than a king—
And admirably schooled in every grace: 10
In fine, we thought that he was everything
To make us wish that we were in his place.

So on we worked, and waited for the light,
And went without the meat, and cursed the bread;
And Richard Cory, one calm summer night,   15
Went home and put a bullet through his head.

QUESTIONS

1. Some critics believe that in the name Richard Cory, Robinson may be alluding to Richard Coeur de Lion (King Richard I, the Lionhearted), who ruled England from 1189 to 1199 and was known for his courage and skill in battle. How does this famous king compare with the poem's title character?

2. How are the point of view and situation ironic? What is the impact on the tone and meaning?

3. Which words in the poem have connotations of royalty or wealth? What do they contribute toward its overall tone?

4. Robinson was famous for his carefully crafted traditional poetry during the late 19th and early 20th centuries, a time of literary experimentation. What does his use of iambic pentameter and regular rhyme contribute to the total effect of the poem?

5. In 1965, Paul Simon altered the poem somewhat and set it to music. Listen to the song and compare it to the original. The audio is available on sites like youtube.com.

Thomas Hardy

The Man He Killed

INTRODUCTION

The Man He Killed

"The Man He Killed," written in 1902 and collected in *Time's Laughingstocks and Other Verses* (1909), focuses on a young soldier's bout with his conscience over having to kill an enemy in the Boer Wars (1880-1881 and 1899-1902). Hardy recognized the innate inhumanity of war and addressed that theme in many of his poems.

Thomas Hardy

English novelist and poet Thomas Hardy was born on June 2, 1840, in Dorset, England, and died on January 11, 1928, at the age of 87. He enjoyed great success and popularity because of such novels as *Far from the Madding Crowd* (1874) and *Tess of the D'Urbervilles* (1891). However, the criticism and outcry over the bare, straightforward realism and occasional pessimism shown in his later novels, especially his last one, *Jude the Obscure* (1895), caused him to concentrate on poetry instead of fiction. His *Wessex Poems* (1898) earned him new respect and helped him continue his career as a writer.

The Man He Killed
Thomas Hardy (1902)

"Had he and I but met
    By some old ancient inn,
We should have sat us down to wet
    Right many a nipperkin!

"But ranged as infantry,   5
    And staring face to face,
I shot at him as he at me,
    And killed him in his place.

"I shot him dead because—
    Because he was my foe,   10
Just so: my foe of course he was;
    That's clear enough; although

"He thought he'd 'list, perhaps,
    Off-hand like—just as I—
Was out of work—had sold his traps—   15
    No other reason why.

"Yes; quaint and curious war is!
    You shoot a fellow down
You'd treat if met where any bar is,
    Or help to half-a-crown."   20

An early Bob Dylan song called "John Brown" includes lyrics similar to the point of Hardy's poem:

"Oh, and I thought when I was there, God, what am I doing here?

I'm a-tryin' to kill somebody or die tryin'

But the thing that scared me most when my enemy came close

And I saw that his face looked just like mine."

Edgar Allan Poe used the phrase "quaint and curious" in the second line of his poem, "The Raven": "...Over many a quaint and curious volume of forgotten lore."

QUESTIONS

1. Why is the poem in quotation marks? To whom do the pronouns in the poem refer?

2. Paraphrase the first stanza. What is its impact on the meaning and tone?

3. What can be inferred from the pause and repeated "because" between lines 1 and 2 in stanza 3?

4. Analyze the irony in stanza 4. What is its effect on the speaker?

5. In the last stanza, Hardy uses an odd word, "quaint," to describe war. What are the denotations, connotations, and effects on the meaning and tone?

6. Identify the rhyme scheme and meter. What part do they have in the overall structure, meaning, and aesthetic impact?

7. State two themes of the poem.

William Wordsworth

The World Is Too Much with Us

INTRODUCTION

The World Is Too Much with Us

Many of Wordsworth's poems are memorable and timeless, as is "The World Is Too Much with Us," published as Sonnet 118 in *Poems in Two Volumes* (1807). The poem criticizes the commercialism and lack of sensitivity that Wordsworth saw as characteristic of the Industrial Revolution. As such, it could be seen as a manifesto for the Romantic Movement, which Wordsworth helped bring to prominence in England.

William Wordsworth

William Wordsworth was one of the founders and leaders, along with Samuel Taylor Coleridge and others, of the Romantic Movement in Britain in the late eighteenth century. Born on April 7, 1770, to a fairly wealthy family in Cumberland, England, he graduated from Cambridge and eventually became the Poet Laureate of England. By that time, however, Wordsworth had nearly stopped writing poetry.

His first sonnet was published when he attended St. John's College in Cambridge. In his Preface to the 1800 edition of *Lyrical Ballads* (first published in 1798), one of the most important works of Romanticism, Wordsworth characterized his poems as "experimental." His poetry often focuses on the simple beauty of nature versus the often ugly world that he encountered, which was created by humans. He traveled extensively and went on long walks during these trips, which furthered his appreciation of nature. Wordsworth died in 1850, after developing a serious inflammation of the lungs.

The World Is Too Much with Us
William Wordsworth (1802)

The world is too much with us; late and soon,
Getting and spending, we lay waste our powers:
Little we see in Nature that is ours;
We have given our hearts away, a **sordid boon**!
The Sea that bares her bosom to the moon,   5
The winds that will be howling at all hours,
And are up-gathered now like sleeping flowers;
For this, for everything, we are out of tune;
It moves us not.—Great God! I'd rather be
A Pagan **suckled** in a creed outworn;   10
So might I, standing on this pleasant **lea**,
Have glimpses that would make me less forlorn;
Have sight of Proteus rising from the sea;
Or hear old Triton blow his wreathéd horn.

The poem is a Petrarchan sonnet with an opening octave and a closing sestet. The rhyme scheme is:

A B B A A B B A   C D C D C D

Sordid: shameful or contemptible

Boon: a benefit or gift

Suckled: nourished, as by a mother

Lea: a field or meadow

"Pagan" refers to any polytheistic religion; the Greeks and Romans were believers in many gods. In Greek mythology, Proteus was a god of the sea who could change his shape whenever he wanted. Triton was another sea god; he was a man with a fish's tail, and he had a large conch shell that he used as a horn, either to calm or disturb the sea, based on the wishes of Poseidon, god of the sea and a brother of Zeus.

QUESTIONS

1. What are the meanings and connotations of the opening statement, lines 1-2?

2. Closely analyze lines 2-4 and discuss what you can infer from them. What is left uncertain?

3. Interpret and explain the language used by Wordsworth in the phrase "sordid boon."

4. Interpret the language used by Wordsworth in lines 5-10. What is the effect on the poem's tone and meaning?

5. What is the controlling metaphor of the poem?

6. How does the traditional structure of the poem contribute to its meaning and aesthetic impact?